ILLINOIS CENTRAL COLLEGE 3

A12901 360087

The Silent Feminists

America's First Women Directors

Anthony Slide

WITHDRAWN

The Scarecrow Press, Inc.
Lanham, Md., and London

I.C.C. LIBRARY

W9-ASJ-667

PN
1998
.2
.S548
1996

SCARECROW PRESS, INC.

Published in the United States of America
by Scarecrow Press, Inc.
4720 Boston Way
Lanham, Maryland 20706

4 Pleydell Gardens, Folkestone
Kent CT20 2DN, England

Copyright © 1996 by Anthony Slide

All rights reserved. No part of this publication may be reproduced,
stored in a retrieval system, or transmitted in any form or by any
means, electronic, mechanical, photocopying, recording, or otherwise,
without the prior permission of the publisher.

British Cataloguing-in-Publication Information Available

Library of Congress Cataloging-in-Publication Data

The silent feminists : America's first women directors / Anthony Slide.
p. cm.
Rev. ed. of : Early women directors. c1977.
Includes bibliographical references and index.
1. Women motion picture producers and directors—United States—
Biography. I. Title.
PN1998.2.S548 1996 791.43'0233'092273—dc20 [B] 96-1178 CIP

ISBN 0-8108-3053-1 (alk. paper)

⊖™ The paper used in this publication meets the minimum requirements of
American National Standard for Information Sciences—Permanence of
Paper for Printed Library Materials, ANSI Z39.48–1984.
Manufactured in the United States of America.

Contents

Introduction

Rediscovering America's First Women Directors

Back in 1972, I was hired to set up and undertake the initial research for the *American Film Institute Catalog: Feature Films, 1911-1920*. As I turned the pages of such early American trade papers as *The Moving Picture World* and *Motion Picture News*, I slowly became aware of the number of films directed by women. Not only were women making films, but contemporary observers were making little of the fact. It was taken for granted that women might direct as often and as well as their male counterparts, and there was no reason to belabor this truth.

The more I read, the more puzzled I became. Why were there so many women directors fifty and sixty years ago and why so few today? Why had their work been so pointedly ignored by critics and historians? The few references in modern books and articles to women in the film industry began with Dorothy Arzner. The interest in women in entertainment did not appear to extend back beyond the coming of sound.

In an effort to correct what I considered to be a considerable wrong, I wrote a slim volume titled *Early Women Directors: Their Role in the Development of the Silent Cinema*, published in 1977 by A. S. Barnes. It sparked some initial interest in the subject and was even published in a German translation. I like to believe that it paved the way for future books and articles on America's first female directors, but at the same time, as the years pass, I am very much aware that little, if any, new research is being undertaken. The facts and opinions I expressed fifteen years ago are simply regurgitated.

When I wrote the book, I concentrated on the careers of Alice Guy Blaché, Lois Weber, Margery Wilson, Frances Marion, Mrs. Wallace Reid, and Dorothy Arzner; I also tried at least to catalog the occasional work of some twenty-five other women active as directors in the American silent-film industry. I felt sure that no one had been missed, but I am still coming across the names of additional women.

The reality of pioneering women directors is one that even the film industry cannot accept with ease. When Richard Attenborough's film biography *Chaplin* was released, it made scant, almost derogatory reference to the comedian's first leading lady, Mabel Normand. There was no mention that she had directed some of Chaplin's first films at Keystone. And Mabel Normand was not alone as a comedienne turned director; in the mid teens, in the course of one year, Gale Henry wrote, directed, produced and co-starred in twenty-six two-reel shorts for Century Comedies. Sidney Drew, one America's best light comedians, starred in films from 1914 until his death in 1919, but it was his wife, billed simply as Mrs. Sidney Drew, who co-directed and constructed the comedies. Dot Farley was a leading lady with Mack Sennett's company, and a few years after Mabel Normand's directorial debut, she also tried her hand at directing.

Women could direct comedy. Women could direct Westerns; in 1917, at Universal, Ruth Ann Baldwin made *'49-'17*. There was no genre that a woman could not tackle and in which a woman was prevented from directing. During the first three decades of its existence, the American film industry was, in many ways, a woman's world. In December 1923, the magazine *The Business Woman*, commented

Excluding acting, considering solely the business possibilities, the positions are held by women in the Hollywood studios as typists, stenographers, secretaries to stars and executives, telephone-operators, hair-dressers, seamstresses, costume-designers, milliners, readers, script-girls, scenarists, cutters, film-retouchers, film-splicers and other laboratory work, set-designers, librarians, artists, title-writers, publicity writers, plaster-molders, casting-directors, musicians, film editors, executives and department-managers, directors, and producers.

When the distinguished publishing house of Houghton Mifflin published a volume on *Careers for Women* in 1920, one chapter was devoted to the occupation of film directing, written by Ida May Park, a prominent Universal screenwriter and director.

Female performers dominated as stars in the silent era, and many headed their own production companies. Mary Pickford was as astute a businesswoman as she was an actress, and she was, of course, the only woman involved in the establishment of the Academy of Motion Picture Arts and Sciences in 1927. With Lillian Gish, Pickford remains one of the icons of the silent screen, a silent star who along with Garbo, Swanson, and a handful of others remains instantly recognizable and identifiable by her last name alone.

Mary Pickford never took credit as a director, but she was obviously heavily involved in the production of her own films, and her directors were hand-picked to follow her commands. At the insistence of her mentor, D. W. Griffith, Lillian Gish did direct one feature film in 1920, *Remodeling Her Husband*, starring sister Dorothy. When Mary Astor came out to the Griffith studios in 1920 to make a screen test, Lillian Gish directed her, thus starting one of the cinema's finest light dramatic actresses on her road to fame.

The concept of women as directors began in France in 1896, when Léon Gaumont permitted his secretary Alice Guy to direct *La Fée aux Choux*, arguably the first fictional film. In France, between 1896 and 1907, Alice Guy directed some 400 films. Subsequently, she married Englishman Herbert Blaché, and the couple came to the United States, where Madame Blaché directed or supervised the production of a further 354 films. In terms of quantity, it is doubtful any other director approached her output. In 1912, she became the first woman to build her own studios and the first American director of either sex to handle such an undertaking. Had it not been for an over-ambitious husband and the need to care for a young daughter, Alice Guy Blaché might have continued directing well into the sound era, but she was forced into retirement in the early 1920s.

Curiously, the name of Gaumont figures prominently in the career of America's first native woman film director, Lois Weber. She first began writing and directing at the American branch of the Gaumont Company in 1908, and she was hired by Herbert Blaché, who was perhaps influenced by his wife's ability in the field. Lois Weber was one of the few genuine auteurs of the American cinema; she always wrote the films which she directed (in the early years she often also starred in them) and used the motion picture as a medium for her ideas and philosophy. At the turn of the century, she had been active in the Church

Army in Pittsburgh, and Weber's attitude toward the cinema was that of a missionary. Although not a Christian Scientist, she embraced many of the ideals of Mary Baker Eddy's religion and spread its gospel in *Jewel* (1915) and *A Chapter in Her Life* (1923). She took on hypocrisy in business, politics, and religion in *Hypocrites* (1915) and fought capital punishment in *The People vs. John Doe* (1916).

Lois Weber was an ardent supporter of Margaret Sanger and the Birth Control Movement. For the day, her views on the subject in *Where Are My Children?* (1916) and *The Hand That Rocks the Cradle* (1917) were outspoken. At the same time, she espoused many middle-class values, including the sanctity of marriage, which she regarded as a partnership. Perhaps because she was *so* middle class and because *Where Are My Children?* is an indictment against abortion, feminists have found it difficult completely to embrace Weber as a pioneering female director. She is certainly deserving of more than a footnote in history.

Like Alice Guy Blaché, Lois Weber opened her own studio, and like Blaché, she had few superiors in the ranks of the male directors. While under contract to Carl Laemmle, she was elected mayor of Universal City, and selected by him to direct the great ballerina Anna Pavlova in her 1916 screen debut, *The Dumb Girl of Portici*. Weber headed a small, but important, band of female directors at Universal in the teens, whose ranks also included Cleo Madison, Ruth Stonehouse, Lule Warrenton, Elsie Jane Wilson, Jeanie MacPherson, and Grace Cunard.

There were many one-shot women directors in the 1920s, but the two women who dominate the decade are Mrs. Wallace Reid and Dorothy Arzner. After drug addiction caused her husband's death in 1923, Mrs. Wallace Reid (the former actress Dorothy Davenport) had no choice but to return to work. Rather than act, she selected to work as a producer and director, initially exploiting her husband's death in *Human Wreckage* (1923) and later making other melodramas, the best of which is *The Red Kimono* (1925).

Dorothy Arzner was a major film editor before Paramount offered her a directorial assignment in 1927 with *Fashions for Women*, a starring vehicle for actress Esther Ralston. *Fashions for Women* and the follow-up feature *Ten Modern Commandments* were minor productions, but they paved the way for Arzner's career in sound films. With Mrs. Wallace Reid, Arzner is the only female director to make the transition to talkies, although Lois Weber was contracted to direct a poverty-row production, *White Heat*, in 1933.

The question that I am most asked, and to which I am unable adequately to respond, is why there were so many women active before the coming of sound and so few after. The answer, in part, lies obviously in the social conditions of the day. When a woman married, it was convention that she cease working, and many female directors chose to retire from the film industry to a life of domesticity. The one exception to this is Lois Weber, who was a major director as long as she was married, but when her husband divorced her, both her life and her career came apart. Another matter which may have played a part in the demise of the woman director was length of service in the industry. Some directors had simply been around too long, and there were no jobs with the coming of sound. The producers had turned for directors to the legitimate stage, which was male dominated at the time.

Also, the industry was changing. In the 'teens, it was easy to make a transition from actress, screenwriter, or editor to director, but by the late 1920s, departmentalization was taking place. There was no easy way to change careers. The advent of the guilds and unions, in the 1930s, further hampered the role of female directors. They were male dominated and remained so through into the 1960s.

As mysterious as the question of why the female director disappeared in the United States is the reason why so little attention has been paid to these pioneering figures in women's history. Perhaps the cause lies in the fact that these women were not feminists and did not espouse feminist issues. Yet by their mere being, they were advancing the rights of women. Women did not have the vote in the United States, but theses individuals in the film industry did have the right to direct—and they seized the opportunity with alacrity.

The major problem in any attempt to rediscover America's first female directors is that the films themselves are missing. Of Alice Guy Blanché's American films, only a handful of the short subjects and only one of the feature films is known to survive. Only one of the three films directed by Frances Marion has been preserved. Margery Wilson is best know for her performance as Brown Eyes in *Intolerance*; she will not be remembered for the films she directed, as none of them exist. Lois Weber directed some forty feature films, but only a dozen can be found in film archives. It is not even the simple matter of the films being lost. An equal problem is that what films have survived are not always the best examples of the director's work. Can we really judge the directorial careers of Cleo Madison and Elsie Jane Wilson on the basis of one film each?

Published documentation helps place the importance of any one female director. We, the audience, must be grateful that at least something has survived, but we must be careful not to be overly judgmental in our viewing of extant works.

Women have come a long way since the days of Alice Guy Blaché and Lois Weber, but at the same time progress has often been retrogressive. Today, the English-speaking

cinema has one brilliant female director in the form of Jane
Campion, but who else do we have with the spirit of
adventure that imbued Alice Guy Blaché and Lois Weber?
We have come far, but not far enough. By viewing the
works of America's first women directors, we will quickly
realize how far we still must go.

My primary reasons in revising and reprinting *Early
Women Directors* under the new title of *The Silent Feminists:
America's First Women Directors* are to provide concise
documentation on the lives and careers of these women
and to offer a general introduction to the subject of women
in the American silent-film industry, an important and
much under-discussed and under-researched topic. The
incentive for the new edition was the completion in 1993
of the documentary feature, *The Silent Feminists: America's
First Women Directors*, which I produced, directed, and
wrote with Jeffrey Goodman. It is ironic that not only was
the first book on women directors in silent films written
by a man, but the first film on the subject was produced
by two men.

I wish I could claim that reaction to the film has been
wildly enthusiastic, but such is far from true. While the
documentary has been well received at film festivals
abroad, purchased for airing on television in many coun-
tries in Europe, South America, Asia, Australasia, and the
Middle East, and made available for home video in the
United Kingdom by Connoisseur Video, *The Silent Feminists* has made little if any impact in the United States. It
has been released for home and educational video use by
Los Angeles-based Direct Cinema and has been screened
in a number of venues. But no screening facility in New
York has expressed any interest in presenting the film; no
major newspaper has reviewed the documentary—indeed
the *Los Angeles Times* refused to review it—and women's
groups appear determined to ignore its existence.

At a Los Angeles reception in 1994, I stood next to a prominent member of the Women in Film organization, a former screenwriter much given to self-promotion. When she asked what I had been doing, I explained I had just returned from the International Women's Film Festival in Creteil, France, where *The Silent Feminists* had been screened some four times and where I had organized a major retrospective on early women directors. "Oh, how interesting," commented the screenwriter as she walked away. Her response is not untypical. I have the distinct impression that many contemporary women filmmakers simply do not want to acknowledge a debt to an earlier generation and have no desire for the record to show that other women were active in the field long before they were even born. As far as most women in film in the 1990s are concerned, the first actress also to produce, write, and direct a film was Barbara Streisand. The names of Lois Weber, Nell Shipman, and others who did precisely these same things more than seventy-five years ago must remain conveniently forgotten. The past is not prologue to what is happening today, but rather a dead topic that should remain buried.

For help in the writing of this and the earlier volume, I would like to thank the staffs of the Margaret Herrick Library of the Academy of Motion Picture Arts and Sciences, the Library of Congress, the literature department of the Los Angeles Central Library, and the Doheny Memorial Library of the University of Southern California. For help in providing biographical documentation, I would like to thank Billy H. Doyle. What few films directed by women I was able to view were in the collections of William K. Everson, the National Film Archive, and most importantly, the Library of Congress.

For their personal reminiscences, I would like to thank the following, most of whom, sadly, are no longer with us: Simone Blaché-Bolton, Priscilla Bonner, Ruth Clifford, Philippe De Lacy, George Folsey, Ethel Grandin, Olga Petrova, Esther Ralston, Mrs. Wallace Reid, Adela Rogers St. Johns, Charles "Buddy" Rogers, Alice Terry, Gilbert Warrenton, and Margery Wilson.

Chapter One

Women and the American Silent Film Industry

"Women's chances of making a living have been increased by the rise of the cinematograph machines," commented the trade paper *The Film Index* in 1908.

Many a young actress anxiously awaiting an engagement will agree to this. At the start, when one concern controlled the production of moving pictures in this country, women helpers were not seriously considered in the plans of managers. As a rule when a woman was needed a man donned petticoats and played the part. Even now in a certain class of pictures this is sometimes done, but generally with pretty poor results. Every year there has been an increased demand for women to pose, and indications are that the demand will go on increasing, for, instead of one concern in the field, there are now fifteen at least. We have no graded scale of pay, and the woman with a beautiful face gets no more than the plainer woman. Action, not looks, is what recommends a woman for employment with us, and the more experienced the applicant the better chance she has. Ingenues are not popular with managers and novices with no stage experience have no show at all.[1]

The writer was, of course, discussing the potential in the early film industry for women as performers, but much of this commentary can be applied to women in all fields of endeavor in the American silent-film industry. Rates of pay were based on experience and skills, not on the sex of the recipient. A pretty face had little relevance to employment possibilities. One need only look at some of the greatest stars of the early years of the film industry—Florence Turner, Mae Marsh, Lillian Gish, and Mary Pickford—to realize that it was not beauty that made an actress a star, but rather striking looks and a strong personality. As to the suggestion that "action" rather than "looks" is of primary importance, the work of serial stars, such as Pearl White, Ruth Roland, Helen Holmes, and Helen Gibson, easily proves the writer's argument. Indeed, the simple fact that all the major serial stars of the silent era were female demonstrates the prominence of women at this time, as opposed to the sound period when the serial stars were men, and women were reduced to simpering and generally incompetent supporting roles.

With the obvious exception of the cowboy stars (whose historical role models were male), the major comedians, and a handful of matinée idols, including Francis X. Bushman and Rudolph Valentino, the stars of the silent screen were female. Actors such as Jack Mulhall or Bryant Washburn served the purpose of leading men to strong feminine stars. Back in the days when being a star meant having one's name above the title of a film, far more women than men held that position. Of the 500 top silent screen performers, including both stars and below-the-title leading players, some 287 were women.

Many female stars had their own production companies, whereas very few actors did. Between 1912 and 1920, there were more than twenty production companies controlled by their female stars. Major names such as Mabel

Normand, Mary Pickford, and Norma Talmadge are found in this number, as well as many obscure and forgotten actresses, including Gail Kane, Marion Leonard, and Virginia Pearson. Yes, it might well be argued that many of the companies were controlled and financed by men, but it was not William Randolph Hearst, Joseph Kennedy, or Joseph M. Schenck whose names "sold" the films to audiences but rather the stars, Marion Davies, Gloria Swanson, and Norma Talmadge. Power was in the name, and the name was woman.

The screen was an extension of the stage, and since the late 1800s women had enjoyed a parity with men in the theater. Backstage, men and women were equal. On tour, actresses handled their own luggage, took care of bills and negotiated contracts no differently than did actors. On the surface it might appear to be unimportant, but as early as 1904, women were allowed to work as ushers in New York theaters. In the theater, women were larger-than-life characters, able to do most things that a man could—including smoking. Curious as it might be in this enlightened age, the fact that women in the theater could, and did, light up a cigarette was a sign of liberation. It was a major breakthrough, if something of a scandal, for the female sex. The story is told of a New York actress stopped by a policeman for smoking with the words, "You can't do that on Fifth Avenue." To which the actress responded, "What do they want women to do, chew?"[2]

The burgeoning film industry did not seek to outrage but rather to be accepted by contemporary audiences. In the early years of the century, nickelodeon theaters began to spring up in their thousands across the United States. They were frowned upon by municipal authorities, and parents discouraged their children from attending performances in the dark, gloomy, and often overcrowded facilities. The industry was quick to realize that women represented respectability. Their presence immediately raised the tone of any nickelodeon theater, and so women were hired as cashiers, front-of-house managers, and pianists to accompany the film. The last were so much a part of the filmgoing experience that by January 21, 1911, Louis Reeves Harrison, a popular writer in the trade paper *The Moving Picture World* was ridiculing them with the collective name of "Lily Limpwrist." On September 2, 1911, *The World* even published a verse on the subject, beginning,

> With a tum-te-tum and an aching thumb
> She keeps the time with her chewing gum.

Women remained prominent as theater managers, and on February 10, 1917, *The New York Dramatic Mirror* published a letter from Miss Alta M. Davis of the Empire Theater, Los Angeles, pointing out that her chosen profession was a great one for her sex:

> It is a known fact that women and children form the greater part of every moving picture audience, and it is but natural that a woman manager should be better qualified than a man to judge the kind of pictures the majority of her patrons like, when most of them are of her own sex. After all the meat in the cocoanut of successful management, so to speak, is in obtaining the right kind of pictures that appeal to the greatest number.

When leading film actress Ormi Hawley announced her retirement in 1921, she was hired by the Panayanakos Brothers to operate three of their movie theaters in Watertown, New York.

Outside of the production arena, theater management was not the only area in which women could be found. In

1909, Frida Klug represented the business interests of various Italian film companies in the United States. In the mid-teens the sales manager for the French-based Eclair Company was a woman, Agnes Egan Cobb. One of the best-known and -liked of early film exchanges was the T. A. Mack Exchange of Chicago, owned and operated by Theresa "Miss Mack" McCaffrey. The exchange handled new and used projectors and accessories, as well as carbons, condensers, tickets, and announcement slides, and apparently, went out of business in 1915.

If a theater in 1913 needed to purchase a poster advertising the latest releases, it would contact Jeanette A. Cohen, responsible for sales at the H. C. Miner Litho Co., and later the Metro Litho Co.

It was little wonder that by 1915, Robert Grau, one of the first serious observers and historians of the film scene was able to write,

> In no line of endeavor has a woman made so emphatic an impress than in the amazing film industry, which has created in its infant stage a new and compelling art wherein the gentler sex is now so active a factor that one may not name a single vocation in either the artistic or business side of its progress in which women are not conspicuously engaged. In the theaters, in the studios and even in the exchanges where film productions are marketed and released to exhibitors, the fair sex is represented as in no other calling to which women have harkened in the early years of the twentieth century.[3]

By 1915, at least three camerawomen, Dorothy Dunn, Grace Davison, and Margaret Ordway, worked in the American film industry, and Louise Lowell was the first newsreel cameraperson under contract to Fox News in

1920. There were also at least five studio managers, Alexia Durant, Nellie Grant, Lillian Greenberger, Annie Marchant, and M. E. Gibson. The last was manager of the Kalem Studio, in Los Angeles, and when it closed in 1917, she became affiliated with the Mabel Condon Exchange, another female-owned establishment. The Canadian-born Gibson had been promoted to studio manager after serving time as secretary to Marshall Neilan, a prominent director who had earlier served as studio manager for Kalem.

The role of the secretary or stenographer in the film industry was discussed in 1923 by *Photoplay*,[4] which pointed out that the position was generally more that of a personal assistant. Famous Players-Lasky first decided to promote some of its stenographers to a new position of "script clerk," the woman who would "hold the script" on the set and was responsible for continuity in filming—a position now called "script girl." It is ironic that in the silent era, producers did not describe their employees as "girls" but instead opted for the sexless description of "clerks."

Among the major secretaries mentioned by *Photoplay* were Margaret Neff (employed by Rudolph Valentino), Josephine Chippo (Wesley Barry), Nellie Bly Baker (Charlie Chaplin), Agnes O'Malley (Richard Walton Tully), Marjorie Jordan (Marshall Neilan), and Gladys Rosson (Cecil B. DeMille). Josephine Chippo became the mistress of director W. S. Van Dyke and wrote the continuity for his 1927 film, *Winners of the Wilderness*. Nellie Bly Baker became an actress and had small roles in Chaplin's *The Kid* (1921) and *A Woman of Paris* (1923).

The scope of work open to women in the film industry ran the gamut from secretary to studio mogul. Directors Alice Guy Blaché and Lois Weber both were heads of their own studios. Mary Pickford co-owned a Hollywood studio with her husband, Douglas Fairbanks, Sr., and as one of the owners of United Artists, she was one of the most powerful businesswomen in America. In 1922, *Photoplay* told the story of "The Girl Picture Magnates,"[5] actress Helen Jerome Eddy and writer Ray Carol, who formed Ray Carol Productions to make their own films for release through Robertson-Cole. On a less grandiose level, in 1914, Katherine F. Carter, who ran the educational division of the General Film Company, founded the Katherine F. Carter Educational and Motion Picture Service Bureau in New York, to lease projection equipment and films for educational use.

Although feminism played little part in the attitudes of women filmmakers to their work, there was an attempt in 1916 to form a feminist film company. Called the American Woman Film Company, it was financed entirely by women, and according to *The Moving Picture World* (May 27, 1916), its intention was "to produce motion pictures of the highest moral and artistic tone." There is no record of the American Woman Film Company actually releasing any productions, and it suffered a major setback on May 23, 1916, when a group of its players and its director, J. Farrell MacDonald, were injured when a truck in which the personnel were traveling crashed at Chatsworth, on the outskirts of Los Angeles. Some twenty-four individuals were hurt, the largest aggregation involved in an accident in the history of the film industry up to that time. The company was returning from location shooting on its first production, *Saul of Tarsus*.

Women were also preeminent in ethnic film production. The Mandarin Film Company, located in 1917 in Oakland, California, had as its president, Marion E. Wong. Described by *The Moving Picture World* (July 7, 1917) as "the only Chinese producing concern in this country," the company released at least one film, *The Curse of Quon Qwon.*

As one glances through trade papers of the period, one is struck by just how many fields of filmmaking boasted at least one woman. Nan Collins was a casting director with United Studios. Prop making is a profession that remains male dominated, but in the 1920s, one woman, Milba Lloyd, worked as a plasterer. In 1921, one of the seven set dressers at the Famous Players-Lasky Studio was a woman name Mary Cutler. Reporting on her work, *Woman's Home Companion* noted, "Girls are learning that if they do not photograph well, they can find something else to do on the motion picture lot, something that keeps them near the film world they love."[6] And let us not forget the women who hand painted each frame of a Pathécolor film, for they were contributing their share to the art of the cinema.

Film editors and cutters were often women, and some of the prominent names from the silent era are Viola Lawrence, Mary O'Connor, Blanche Sewell, and Rose Smith (who edited *The Birth of a Nation* and other D. W. Griffith films with her husband, James). Irene Morra was both a major film editor and a production manager in the 1920s. Margaret Booth began her career as a cutter with D. W. Griffith, working on *Orphans of the Storm* (1921), before becoming the preeminent film editor at M-G-M.

"Among the greatest 'cutters' and film editors are women," editorialized *Motion Picture Magazine* in November 1925. "They are quick and resourceful. They are also ingenious in their work and usually have a strong sense of what the public wants to see. They can sit in a stuffy cutting-room and see themselves looking at the picture before an audience."

The fan magazine continued,

Women writers may also be said to dominate the scenario field. There is a deep scientific reason for this. Some years ago a series of psychological experiments were made in a German university town— long before motion pictures were heard of. School children of both sexes were required to write fiction stories. One fact was established as a result of the experiment; the girl children were not so logical in their plots; they didn't bother so much how they "got there"; but they showed a superior sense of picturization to the boy children. Also their stories had more interesting detail and more sentiment and more emotion.

So it would seem that women were naturally fitted for the work of writing for the screen. Experience of motion picture companies has shown that the combination of a woman, with her quick, alert sense of invention and her ability to "see in pictures," and a director with a logical sense of construction, is the ideal working team for movies.[7]

While the described German experiment might be doubtful as to its authenticity, there is no question that some of the best-known screenwriters during the silent era were women and that they wielded considerable power. In 1918 alone, some forty-four women were employed in the film industry as scenario writers — compared to thirty-six in 1933. Aside from actually writing scenarios, women were to be found in related areas. For example, the first head of the Vitagraph Company's scenario department was a Mrs. Beta Breuil, of whom nothing is known.

While it might be difficult to come up with a list of male screenwriters from the silent era, it is relatively easy to produce a listing of their female equivalents: Clara S. Beranger, Ouida Bergère, Sada Cowan, Beulah Marie Dix,

Dorothy Farnum, Bradley King, Anita Loos, Josephine Lovett, June Mathis, Bess Meredyth, Olga Printzlau, Margaret Turnbull, Eve Unsell, and Dorothy Yost. In *The Moving Picture World* (August 24, 1918), Clara S. Beranger argued that women were better scriptwriters:

> It needs no cursory glance at the current releases and those of even six months ago to prove that there are more writers among the feminine sex than the male persuasion.
>
> The heart throb, the human interest note, child life, domestic scenes and even the eternal triangle is more ably handled by women than men because of the thorough understanding our sex has of these matters. It is an old truism that love to a woman is her whole existence, while to the man it is a mere incident in his life. This is one of the reasons why a woman writing drama for the screen gives to her story the sincerity that no man can lend. With this sincerity the audience gets plausibility and probability. Men writers in developing their story have to create artificial emotions which they delude themselves into believing is inspiration.

Of course, Beranger is using a form of reverse sexism to argue her point, but that does not invalidate what she has to say. It is not the film industry but outside forces, the climate of the times, that dictates an attitude of mind. At the same time that attitude of mind could be altered through the power of the motion picture. Just as women were first brought into the film industry to enforce respectability, Hollywood again turned to women in the early 1920s when various scandals—including the William Desmond Taylor murder and the accusation of rape against Roscoe "Fatty" Arbuckle—threatened its well-being. "Refinement without undue prudishness—that is what the movies are waiting for the women to bring them," argued *Illustrated World* in 1923.[8] The industry knew that its audience was primarily female and that to turn the spotlight on the women holding prominent positions in filmmaking might dilute some of the harsh criticism from across the country. "Records show that about three-fourths of matinee audiences or even a larger percentage are woman," wrote Irving Thalberg.

> Women do not take their entertainment passively. They are good "word-of-mouth" advertisers, and they are usually the means of bringing their husbands and families to the theatre. That is why I say that pictures should be made primarily for the feminine mind. A picture that will please women will please men, but the reverse cannot be counted upon....Women are dominant among the theatre-going public.[9]

The film industry needed to manipulate the minds of its female audience. It did so through the fan magazines and their gossip writers, through women such as Adela Rogers St. Johns, Ruth Waterbury, Hazel Simpson Naylor, Gladys Hall, Myrtle Gebhart, Adele Whitely Fletcher, and, of course, Louella Parsons (who began her career in the teens), who not only wrote for, but also edited the fan magazines of the silent era. First National Pictures even published a newssheet, titled *Fashions and Fillers for Feminine Fans*. In it, Constance Talmadge "wrote" on "Opportunities for Women in Motion Pictures." One issue was devoted to the work of Ruth Oelman, a location finder, who told Ms. Talmadge, "It is wonderfully interesting work, it brings you in contact with such a wide variety of people, and the satisfaction one feels when a location has been found, which will later help towards the success of some great picture, is unsurpassable." Another issue featured the publicity writer, represented by Beulah Livingstone, who thought "publicity is the coming game of women," and who was responsible for promoting the career of dramatic star Norma Talmadge.

Margaret McWade was a prominent film critic for the trade paper *The Moving Picture World* in the teens. Later film critics from the 1920s included Mary Boyle (*Photoplay*), Lillian W. Brennan (*The Film Daily*), Mary Jane Warren (*Motion Pictures Today*), and Delight Evans (*Screenland*). In the 1920s, M-G-M's preeminent studio portrait photographer was a woman, Ruth Harriet Louise, who photographed Lon Chaney, John Gilbert, Lillian Gish, and Greta Garbo and still awaits recognition and a place among her peers such as Clarence Sinclair Bull and George Hurrell.

With the end of the silent era, women continued in prominence in a number of areas of filmmaking, but not as directors. In 1929, *Ladies' Home Journal* reported,

Nowadays no woman with a hidden longing—or the necessity to earn a living—need despair. She may not have the talent or training to become an artist or a writer, a physician or a lawyer, but she can always be a cooper or a constable, an auctioneer or an undertaker, a professional packer or a teacher of jujitsu, a stonemason or a plasterer, a longshoreman or a lifeguard, a railroad porter or a policeman. Other women are doing all these things and many more besides; in fact, of the 572 gainful occupations listed by the United States Census Bureau in 1920, only thirty-five had not yet been invaded by the gentle sex. And that was eight years ago.[10]

The role of women in American society was expanding, but in the film industry, their importance—except as stars—was diminishing. While employment opportunities opened up in all fields across the United States, the role of film director was taken away from women. Once the industry became too successful and no longer needed to seek respectability, it could disregard and discard its female employees—no matter how talented they might be—and become a male-dominated business.

Notes

1 . "Women Film Actors," *The Film Index*, vol. III, no. 38, October 3, 1908, p. 9.

2. This story is told in Philip S. Lewis, *Trouping*, New York: Harper and Row, 1973, p. 121.

3. Robert Grau, "Woman's Conquest in Filmdom," *Motion Picture Supplement*, September 1915, p. 41.

4. Lois Hutchinson, "A Stenographer's Chance in Pictures," *Photoplay*, vol. XXIII, no. 4, March 1923, pp. 42-43, 107.

5. Joan Jordan, "The Girl Picture Magnates," *Photoplay*, vol. XXII, no. 3, August 1922, pp. 23, 111.

6. Quoted in Anne Walker, "The Girls Behind the Screen," *Woman's Home Companion*, vol. XLVIII, no. 1, January 1921.

7. Florence M. Osborne, "Why Are There No Women Directors?" *Motion Picture Magazine*, vol. XXX, no. 4, November 1925, p. 5.

8. E. Leslie Gilliams, "Will Woman Leadership Change the Movies?" *Illustrated World*, February 1923, p. 860.

9. Irving G. Thalberg, "Women—and the Films," *The Film Daily*, vol. XXVII, no. 70, June 22, 1924, p. 29.

10. Ann Hark, "Jills of All Trades," *Ladies' Home Journal*, February 1929, p. 10.

Chapter Two

Alice Guy Blaché

To have been a pioneering woman filmmaker is a major accomplishment in its own right, but Alice Guy Blaché was not just the first of her sex to direct a film, she was also one of the first individuals of either sex to make films on a regular basis. While film directing was an unknown profession for a man, Alice Guy Blaché was turning out productions on a regular basis. In the United States, the earliest filmmakers were male and were cinematographers first and foremost. While she had a thorough knowledge and understanding of the mechanics of cinematography, Alice Guy Blaché left the handling of the camera to others and virtually single-handedly established the concept of the director as a separate entity in the filmmaking process. As *Photoplay* wrote of her in 1912, Alice Guy Blaché was "a striking example of the modern woman in business who is doing a man's work. She is doing successfully what men are trying to do. She is succeeding in a line of work in which hundreds of men have failed."[1]

This remarkable woman was born Alice Guy on July 1, 1873 at Saint-Mandé, on the outskirts of Paris, into a comfortable, middle-class family.[2] She spent her early years in Chile, where her father was a businessman, but was educated at convent schools in France; her mother encouraged her to take typing and stenography lessons in the hope that her daughter would become self-supporting. In 1894 and 1895, Alice Guy was hired as a secretary by Léon Gaumont, then owner of a successfully photographic concern in Paris. When Gaumont became involved in cinematography in 1896, Alice Guy asked if she might be allowed to make films. Since Gaumont—like Thomas Edison in the United States —considered cinematography little more than a child's toy, he had no objection to her doing as she wished—on the understanding that her film-making activities should not interfere with her secretarial duties. So in 1896, Alice Guy wrote, directed, and photo-graphed, with the help of her friend and sister-secretary Yvonne Serand, a short subject titled *La Fée aux Choux* (or *The Cabbage Fairy*).

"I should exaggerate if I told you it was a masterpiece," wrote Alice Guy in her autobiography, "but the public then was not jaded, the actors were young and pleasing, and the film had enough success that I was allowed to try again."[3]

Alice Guy continued as a film director with the blessing and financial support of Léon Gaumont. Apparently, every motion picture produced by Gaumont up through 1905 was directed by Alice Guy. In that year, needing assistance, she hired Ferdinand Zecca as a director, Victo-rin Jasset as an assistant, and Louis Feuillade as a writer. In so doing, it was as if, with one mighty stroke, she had single-handedly created the entire French film industry. Of the more than 400 short subjects that she made, it would be difficult to single out individual productions. One of the best known, and one of the longest—running some 600 meters—is *La Vie du Christ* (also known as *The Passion Play*), originally released in March 1906. As did D. W. Griffith in making the Judaean sequence in *Intolerance*, Alice Guy used as her source the illustrations from the James Tissot Bible.

Like Thomas Edison, Léon Gaumont experimented with sound motion pictures, but while the American discarded his efforts fairly early, only to revive them in a half-hearted and unsuccessful fashion in 1911, Gaumont continually promoted his "Chronophone" system, exhibiting it as early as 1901 at the St. Louis World's Fair. Because the sound could only be recorded when the speaker was close to the equipment, it was necessary to record the sound first and then have the players mouth back to a recording, but by 1911 Gaumont had solved the problem sufficiently to permit the taking of sound and picture simultaneously, with the players up to a distance of twenty-five feet from the equipment.

Gaumont, of course, deserves full credit for the invention of the Chronophone, but it was Alice Guy who directed the first films for the system, giving her the dubious distinction of being the first person in the world to direct sound motion pictures.

The Chronophone led to Alice Guy's coming to the United States. In 1906, a young Englishman named Herbert Blaché-Bolton (1882-1953) was sent to learn the technicalities of filmmaking at the Gaumont plant. He and Alice Guy worked together, shooting on location, and at Christmas, 1906, they became engaged. Early in 1907, the couple were married, and three days later they sailed for the United States to work with two entrepreneurs in Cleveland, Ohio, who had acquired the U.S. rights to the Chronophone.

Upon arrival in America, it was decided to drop "Bolton" from their name and henceforth, the two were known as Alice Guy and Herbert Blaché. In Cleveland, Alice Guy Blaché became a housewife, and in 1908 she gave birth to her daughter, Simone. Blaché set up offices at the Electric Building in Cleveland, but the two Americans who had acquired the Chronophone system, George B. Pettingill and Max Faetkenheuer, proved unable to market it successfully, with the latter declaring bankruptcy early in 1908. The rights to the Chronophone process reverted back to Léon Gaumont, and in the summer of 1908 Herbert Blaché and his family moved to New York. Blaché became manager of the New York office of Gaumont, at 124 East 25th Street, and established a temporary studio for the Gaumont Chronophone at Flushing, New York, in the summer of 1909. Films produced using the Chronophone process were not screened in New York until June 1913, at the 39th Street Theater, in partnership with a program of Gaumont Chronochrome or color shorts.

As Alice Guy Blaché recorded in her autobiography, "The Gaumont studio was not being used every day. The temptation was too strong; I resolved to rent it and try making a few films."[4] With her husband, Alice Guy Blaché founded the Solax Company on September 7, 1910, with herself as president and director-in-chief. From 1910 through June 1914, when Solax ceased to exist, Madame Blaché was to supervise the direction of every one of the company's 331 films, the bulk of which were one-reel (or ten minutes) in length. The first Solax film, shot at 46-64 Congress Avenue (later to be known as 137th Street and Latimer Place), Flushing, New York, was *A Child's Sacrifice*, released on October 21, 1910, and starring Magda Foy, billed as "The Solax Kid."

Foy was a member of the stock company of players that Madame Blaché developed at Solax, which also included Darwin Karr (who joined the company in November 1911), Vinnie Burns, Marian Swayne, Blanche Cornwall, Claire Whitney, Billie Quirk, Lee Beggs, and Fraunie Fraunholz. While not untalented in comparison with performers at other studios of the period, none of the Solax players enjoyed starring careers in later years.

In 1912, Alice Guy Blaché decided it was time to move to a new studio and she decided to custom build one in Fort Lee, New Jersey, becoming the first and only woman to erect her own studio. The glass-enclosed structure was completed in September 1912; it was destroyed by fire on January 6, 1923. Extraordinary as it might be, while planning the studio and supervising production of more than 100 films in a one-year period, Alice Guy Blaché also found time, in 1912, to give birth to a second child, Reginald.

Photoplay described the director at work:

She quietly moves about the plant, unostentatiously and unobtrusively energetic. She carries with her an air of refinement and culture, and her dark, modest clothes bespeak and emphasize her dignity. This dignity, however, never borders on frigidity. She smiles encouragingly upon every one she meets. Her commands are executed to the letter with dispatch and efficiency, not because she is feared, but because she is liked. Although Madame Blaché has decided ideas, and at times will obstinately insist that they be carried out, she is always too willing to listen to suggestions. She is not a woman who is amenable to flattery. Unlike other women in business, she is really the first sometimes to see her own errors and will often, with resentment, admit the justice of criticism.[5]

A fascinating personal glimpse of the Solax Studio was provided by Frank Leon Smith:

When I worked in the Pathé-Astra Studio in Jersey City her name [Alice Guy Blaché] was often spoken by my French bosses. They respected her, but, I think, also resented a woman succeeding as a writer, director, and producer of movies. One day I was sent to go over a script with a Pathé director working at Madame Blaché's glass-roofed Solax studio at Fort Lee. The big stage was empty at the time, and Madame Blaché was not there, but high on one wall, in letters two feet tall, was her mandate, "Be Natural." She had put this sign up for the guidance of the young and inept, self-conscious extras, and old pros (actors) addicted to stage tricks the camera could turn into farce, and it spoke to *me*, a confused young fellow— Her sign was amazing for those times, when the common phrase for acting in movies was "posing for pictures. "[6]

It is obviously physically impossible for Alice Guy Blaché to have directed all the Solax productions. In no way does it take away from her record as a pioneer and as production head of the company to acknowledge that others must have had a hand in the direction of some of the Solax films. One individual known to have worked at Solax as a director is Edward Warren. Born in Boston in 1857, Warren joined Solax in the summer of 1911 after a lengthy stage career. He had gained experience as a theatrical actor and director with Charles and Daniel Frohman, Klaw & Erlanger, and others. In contemporary publicity, Warren took credit for *The Equine Spy* (1912), *Dublin Dan* (1912), *Beasts of the Jungle* (1913), *Kelly from the Emerald Isle* (1913), and *Brennan of the Moor* (1913), the last three of which were all major Solax productions. Of course he directed many, many more.

Edward Warren resigned from Solax in July 1913 in order to direct a seven-reel feature on the Boy Scouts of America. The film did not receive a general release until 1915, under the title of *The Adventures of a Boy Scout*. It was probably shot at the Solax Studio. In 1917, Warren formed his own company, Edward Warren Productions, and directed three feature films with wildly melodramatic titles, *Weavers of Life* (1917), *The Warfare of the Flesh* (1917), and *Thunderbolts of Fate* (1918). To survive, Warren would take occasional acting roles on screen. He died in Los Angeles on April 3, 1930.

One of the first major Solax productions was *The Violin Maker of Nuremberg*, released on December 22, 1911. It was the tale of two apprentice violin makers (played by Berkeley Barrington and Gladden James), who both were in love with their master's daughter (Blanche Cornwall). A violin-making contest is held to determine who will win the girl, but the better of the two, knowing that she really loves his rival, substitutes his violin for his colleague's. *The Moving Picture World* (December 9, 1911) commented, "It is a story of tender sentiment told amid scenes of artistic quaintness. It carries a simple sentimental thread in a skillful manner that never descends to the commonplace, and, at the same time, holds the interest with its dignity and artistic charm." Madame Blaché's daughter, Simone, had a small role in the film and also appeared in others, including *Blood and Water*, released on June 4, 1913.

There is no linking theme to the Solax productions. There are simply too many for Alice Guy Blaché to have concentrated on a single philosophical thought or subject matter. The handful of Solax films that are extant illustrate a strong understanding of filmmaking techniques of the period but have no great creative sweep. Technically the films are on a par with those made by Madame Blaché's male counterparts, and she is willing to experiment, as in *Beasts of the Jungle*, with its split screen, or *Canned Harmony* (released on October 9, 1912), with its triple-screen effect. The latter is of more than passing interest in that its thematic use of a musician performing to a playback is remindful of Blaché's Chronophone films, and the use of slang expressions in the titles demonstrates that the director had come to terms with her sojourn in the United States. The triple-screen effect is not just there to demonstrate Blaché's cleverness but serves a distinct purpose as the suitor talks to his girlfriend on the telephone, he at left, she at right, while the shot of the empty road in the middle frame signifies the distance between them and their hopes of marriage.

A viewing of the surviving Solax films shows that Madame Blaché was most adept at comedy. The humor is not slapstick in nature, but often coy and subtle. *The Detective's Dog*, released on April 10, 1912, is an amusing satire on early melodrama, with a dog racing to the rescue of his master who is about to be cut in half on a sawmill. Here is one of the great classic clichés of early silent melodrama—presented *as* a cliché—and only a filmmaker with a firm grasp of her craft could get away with it! *A House Divided*, released on May 2, 1913, is a comedy of domestic strife, a precursor to the charming domestic comedies of a few years later that were to be made by Mr. and Mrs. Sidney Drew and Mr. and Mrs. Carter De Haven. Husband and wife suspect each of infidelity, and the family lawyer only adds to the problems. Fraunie Fraunholz is excellent as the husband, but it is the character actresses, playing the secretary and the housekeeper who provide the broad humor.

Matrimony's Speed Limit, released on June 11, 1913, is similar in plotline to Buster Keaton's *Seven Chances*, complete with a racist joke. It is curious that *Seven Chances*, released in 1925, is based on a 1924 farce, which makes one wonder if the author of the latter could possibly have seen *Matrimony's Speed Limit*. As evidence of just how primitive filmmaking could be, even in 1913, Solax could not bother to give the title in full on the film itself; it is called simply *Matrimony's S.L.*

By 1913, Solax was producing a number of three-reel productions. From 1912 onwards, Solax released its films as an independent producer, through the Mutual Film Corporation, but these multi-reel offerings would appear to have been sold directly by Solax on a states rights basis. The first of the major films was *Beasts of the Jungle*, released on January 11, 1913. It starred child actress Vinnie Burns and featured a fight between Paul Bourgeois and a lion. Vinnie Burns was seen as Dick in *Dick Whittington and His Cat*, released on March 1, 1913. In *The New York Dramatic Mirror* (March 5, 1913), Solax claimed that the production boasted a cast of 200 and twenty-six sets, and cost an estimated $35,000. The popular Irish actor Barney Gilmore was the star of *Dublin Dan*, released on October 9, 1912, *Kelly from the Emerald Isle*, released on May 17, 1913, and *Brennan of the Moor*, released in August 1913. In announcing *Kelly from the Emerald Isle*, *The Moving Picture News* (May 10, 1913) reported that "the sales on the *Beasts of the Jungle* and *Dick Whittington*...have been a phenomenal success. For these features, they have sold nearly every state in the Union and some of the states they could have sold three times over."

One may guage the importance of Alice Guy Blaché at this time through a feature in the February 17, 1912, issue of the *New York Clipper*. "Prominent Independent Film Manufacturers" were asked to comment on the industry. Madame Blaché is the second filmmaker to be listed, preceded only by Carl Laemmle, then president of the IMP Company and shortly to be head of Universal Pictures. Madame Blaché told the *Clipper*:

I have always believed in clean pictures; pictures which educate as well as entertain. In directing the producing policy of my company I have always impressed upon my associate directors that success comes only to those who give the public what it wants, plus something else. That something else I would call our individuality, if you please.

I have long recognized the great influence that can be exerted by the motion picture on the public mind. I have always felt that pictures will recommend themselves to the public on their educational merits. The days of the unclean pictures are gone. I personally have always condemned them.

Our policy to-day, which I have instituted, is to produce as many high-class educational pictures and comedies of the refined type as we are able to secure. At present there is a dearth in good educational pictures and in refined comedy scenarios.

Solax ceased functioning as a production entity early in 1914. The reason why is not totally clear, but it would seem to be connected to the advent of the feature film—up to that time, Solax had produced only two feature films of four reels (the minimum length), *Ben Bolt* (1913) and *Beneath the Czar* (1914) — and the company name was inexorably linked to short subjects rather than features. Solax was also inexorably linked to Alice Guy Blaché, and this may well have caused jealousy on the part of her husband. Up until the spring of 1913, Herbert Blaché was still Gaumont's representative in the United States — its vice-president — and he could hardly devote his time to another company. When he resigned from Gaumont, he established Blaché Features, in October 1913, and persuaded his wife to become part of the new organization, under his supervision.

Jealousy on the part of Herbert Blaché played a prominent part in the ultimate downfall of Alice Guy Blaché. Unquestionably, she was the better director, but Blaché would never accept that reality. In trade paper advertising, he routinely advertised himself and his services above those of his wife. On some films, Blaché would even insist that his wife take on the duties of his assistant director, which lowered her status in the film community and obviously affected her potential for employment by independent producers who would want a qualified director, not an assistant, to handle their films.

The first release of Blaché Features—on November 17, 1913—was the four-reel, *The Star of India*, featuring Fraunie Franholz and Claire Whitney (evidence of the close connection between Blaché Features and Solax), and directed by Herbert Blaché. It was not well received. *The New York Dramatic Mirror* (December 31, 1913) commented,

> This is a four-reel melodramatic offering that staggers our credence. There is but one girl in the play, but the villains and the counter-villains and the hero as well, make the most of her that they can. The action around the girl entirely supersedes the quest of the Star of India—a valuable diamond—for over two reels, there being times when we almost forgot, and care less, about the whereabouts of that precious stone.

It is well to compare the latter review with one from *The Moving Picture World* (March 21, 1914) of Alice Guy Blaché's first film for Blaché Features, *The Dream Woman*, released in March 1914:

> In making the picture, the producer has discarded all except what she needed for her peculiar effect. But the telling quality of the picture comes most from the fact that, by the mysterious alchemy of art she changed what material she did use into something her own, fresh, new, life-like of today.

Through its existence, approximately half of the productions of Blaché Features were directed by Madame Blaché. Blaché Features was followed by a new company, again promoted by her husband, the U.S. Amusement Company, which released through Art Dramas. Most of its productions were directed by Herbert Blaché. A few, including *The Adventurer*, based on a story by Upton Sinclair and released on February 15, 1917, were directed by Alice Guy Blaché. It is worth noting her continued reputation as evidenced by the following comment from *The Moving Picture World* (March 24, 1917): "this reviewer has yet to see a picture by Madame Blaché that was not sincerely and artistically directed and this, *The Adventurer*, one of her recent productions, is no exception."

During this period, Madame Blaché was primarily employed by New York-based Popular Plays and Players, which released its films through Alco, a subsidiary of Metro Pictures. Here she directed five features starring Olga Petrova, including her screen debut. Madame Petrova was a British-born (Muriel Harding) dramatic actress and vaudeville headliner with a strong feminist streak. She would only play dominant women on screen and could be temperamental. But the two women worked well together, and, in later years, Madame Petrova recalled, "Looking back again I retain for her the same reactions of deep affection and respect as I had for her so many years ago."[7] The Blaché-Petrova relationship began with *The Tigress*, released on December 7, 1914, followed by *The Heart of a Painted Woman* (1915), *The Vampire* (1915), *My Madonna* (1915), and *What Will People Say?* (1916).

Madame Blaché's last two films, both for Pathé release, were *The Great Adventure*, released on March 10, 1918, and *Tarnished Reputations*, released on March 14, 1920. The former was Bessie Love's first film for Pathé and marked Flora Finch's return to the screen. Love's performance drew praise; as *Exhibitor's Trade Review* (March 2, 1918) noted, "It is her pleasing acting that pulls the rather unappealing story out of the rut and gives it the stamp of an accomplished production."

Tarnished Reputations featured Dolores Cassinelli, and was not too great a critical success. *Exhibitor's Trade Review* (April 9, 1920) described it as "five reels of anguish." Commented *Variety* (April 9, 1920), "The story is by Leonce Perret and has a French melodramatic slant to it that is a little off the average of good American stuff. Mme. Alice Blaché directed. Neither of these experts are naturally adapted to bringing Miss Cassinelli those qualities that would put her at the top."

Madame Blaché was offered the direction of *Tarzan of the Apes*, but declined that dubious honor. Why did her film career end? In part, it was due to Herbert Blaché's interference in her work and his open infidelity, particularly with actress Catherine Calvert. As her daughter, Simone, noted, Alice Guy Blaché was extremely French, and she was also extremely nineteenth century. The ways of the American film industry were not her ways. She could not turn a blind and unforgiving eye to what her husband was doing. Further, although none of her features are extant, except for one that is unavailable for viewing, it seems probable that Alice Guy Blaché was being left behind as the industry advanced into the 1920s and a new decade of sophistication in filmmaking. She belonged to the past, to the cinema's infancy, and perhaps found it difficult to come to grips with a new generation of young filmmakers and film performers with new ideas and a new morality.

By 1922, Alice Guy Blaché and her husband had separated, and Madame Blaché returned to France. In the late 1920s, she tried, without success, to become involved in film production. She worked as a translator and attempted, yet again unsuccessfully, to sell a book for children that she had authored and illustrated. She lived in France, Switzerland, Belgium, and the United States, with her daughter Simone, who had become a secretary with the American Foreign Service. Eventually, Madame Blaché suffered a stroke; she died in New Jersey—the state in which she had spent virtually all her years of American filmmaking—on March 24, 1968.

Alice Guy Blaché might have entered films on a casual basis, but unlike later American women directors, she was quick to recognize the potential that the motion picture held for her sex. In 1914, she wrote on "Woman's Place in Photoplay Production." She was also one of the first to acknowledge that film might one day become an academic subject, and on July 13 and August 3, 1917, she lectured to students at New York's Columbia University. She was a very unique and original human being.

Notes

1. H. Z. Levine, "Madame Alice Blaché," *Photoplay*, vol. II, no. 2, March 1912, p. 38. It must be acknowledged that the author of this complimentary piece was a paid publicist for Solax.

2. Simone Blaché believes the correct year is 1875.

3. Anthony Slide, editor, *The Memoirs of Alice Guy Blaché*, translated by Roberta and Simone Blaché, Metuchen, NJ: Scarecrow Press, 1986, p. 26.

4. Ibid, p. 62.

5. H. Z. Levine, "Madame Alice Blaché," *Photoplay*, vol. II, no. 2, March 1912, p. 38.

6. Letter in *Films in Review*, vol. XV, no. 4, April 1964, pp. 254-255.

7. Undated letter to Anthony Slide.

Chapter Three

Lois Weber

"When the history of the dramatic early development of motion pictures is written, Lois Weber will occupy a unique position," wrote Aline Carter in *Motion Picture Magazine* in 1921.

Associated with the work since its infancy, she has set a high pace in its growth, for not only is she a producer of some of the most interesting and notable productions we have had, but she writes her own stories and continuity, selects her casts, directs the pictures, plans to the minutist detail all the scenic effects, and, finally, titles, cuts and assembles the film. Few men have assumed such a responsibility.[1]

Along with D. W. Griffith, Lois Weber was the American cinema's first genuine auteur, a filmmaker involved in all aspects of production and one who utilized the motion picture to put across her own ideas and philosophies. A gentle propagandist who became an advocate on a variety of subjects, including the abolition of capital punishment, an end to hypocrisy in American life and society, a recognition of the value of teachers, and, above all, the right of women to access birth control procedures, Lois Weber was unique in American film history. America's first native-born woman filmmaker, Lois Weber was also the most important female director to have worked in the film industry throughout its existence, and the only one to set her own agenda as to her productions and their contents.

Lois Weber's films took moral stands on a variety of controversial issues. In *The Hypocrites* (1914), she told a story of religious hypocrisy and used it as a backdrop to consider hypocrisy in marriage and political corruption. The hypocrisy of the scandalmongers was examined in *Scandal* (1915). At a time when even the distribution of information on birth control was subject to prosecution, Weber made two films, *Where Are My Children?* (1916) and *The Hand That Rocks the Cradle* (1917), strongly advocating birth control but taking a stand against abortion. Police methods to obtain a confession and the question of capital punishment were dealt with in *The People vs. John Doe* (1916). Drug addiction and racial and religious prejudice were other topics that this fearless woman tackled in her films over a career that extended from 1908 through into the 1930s.

While not a Christian Scientist, Weber did advocate the principles of that religion as early as 1912 in *The Power of Thought*. She also filmed two versions of a Clara Louise Burnham novel that promoted Christian Science, *Jewel* (1915) and *A Chapter in Her Life* (1923). Just as Mary Baker Eddy was the only woman to found a major religion, Lois Weber was the only woman in the American film industry to become as important a film director as any man. Yet both are ignored by feminists and the women's movement, because the politics and backgrounds of each do not fit a convenient mold of Leftist thought and behavior.

Lois Weber had worked with the Church Army in Pittsburgh at the turn of the century, and she saw her work in the film industry as that of a missionary. Using motion pictures, she could reach a far greater number than might hear what she had to say in dingy church halls or underpopulated congregations. She set out to convert to her viewpoint not only film audiences but also members of the film community. In 1913, speaking on the topic of "The Making of Picture Plays That Will Have an Influence for Good on the Public Mind," Weber told the Woman's City Club of Los Angeles:

> During two years of Church Army work I had ample opportunity to regret the limited field any individual worker could embrace even by a life of strenuous endeavor. Meeting with many in that field who spoke strange tongues, I came suddenly to realize the blessing of a voiceless language to them. To carry out the idea of missionary pictures was difficult. To raise the standard was a different matter, but the better class of producers were prompt in trying to do this when they were brought to a realization of defects by censorship. It took years to interest the best actors and to bring back refined audiences, but even this has been accomplished. We need thoughtful men and women to send us real criticisms and serious communications regarding our efforts.[2]

Lois Weber might be religious, but it should not be assumed that she was prudish or conservative in her outlook. She was a fierce opponent of censorship, speaking often on the subject. In *The Hypocrites*, she used an actress to represent "The Naked Truth" and photographed her in full frontal nudity, in a fashion that would outrage much of American society in the 1990s. She was an intellectual, who looked to magazines and newspapers for many of the ideas for her films. After reading an editorial in the March 21, 1915 issue of the Los Angeles *Sunday Examiner* on the poisonous and dangerous nature of gossip, she wrote the script for *Scandal*. An article on

"Impoverished College Teaching" in the April 30, 1921 issue of *Literary Digest* led her to make *The Blot* (1921), in which she points out the poverty of college professors and the clergy and the need to pay as much to those who clothe our minds as we are willing to pay to the tradespeople who clothe our bodies.

On June 13, 1879, Lois Weber was born in Allegheny (now part of Pittsburgh), Pennsylvania. Her family encouraged her to become a concert pianist, but stage fright ended her career after only a year, and Weber decided to study voice in New York in the hope of returning to the stage as an actress. She worked as a soubrette, and while appearing in the touring company of a musical play titled *Why Girls Leave Home*, she met Phillips Smalley (1875 - 1939), the stage manager. The couple married in 1905 and Smalley was to be a tremendous, supportive influence in Weber's career. His name appears alongside Lois Weber's as her co-director on most of the films through the late 'teens. When the couple was divorced in 1922, Weber went to pieces, and her career seemed at an end. While she did not need Phillips Smalley in a an intellectual or practical sense, she needed him on an emotional level, to assure her in what she did and to offer support when support was needed. His name next to hers on the credits of a film in no fashion takes away from Lois Weber's importance as a director or her work as the sole creative producer of the film.

As had Alice Guy Blaché before, Lois Weber began her film career with Gaumont. She and Phillips Smalley joined the American-based Gaumont Chronophone Company in 1908, directing, acting in, and in Weber's case writing, a considerable number—Weber in later years suggested the figure ran into the hundreds—of early sound-on-disc films. Alice Guy Blaché was the first individual, male or female, to direct a sound motion picture—Lois Weber was the second. In 1915, Weber recalled,

> I was fortunate in being associated with broad-minded men. Both Mr. Smalley and Mr. Blaché listened to my suggestions. They approved or disapproved as the suggestions were good or bad, and I did the same with the ones they offered. The work became a real pleasure when we brought our individual talents into an effective combination, and we were enabled to turn out many original and successful photoplays. That is the way I acquired my first experience in arranging the drama for the screen. Our combination worked in perfect harmony, and would have continued to the present day but for the natural growth of the organization.[3]

From Gaumont, Weber and Smalley moved on to the Reliance Motion Picture Company in 1910. When Edwin S. Porter founded the Rex Company, the couple became its resident directors and leading players, turning out an average of one film a week. When Rex became a subsidiary of Universal Pictures in 1912, Weber and Smalley became its production heads, answerable only to Universal president, Carl Laemmle. At Universal, Lois Weber's career blossomed. She directed, wrote, and starred in an average of one short film a week, with the emphasis on the drama. On November 29, 1913, *The Universal Weekly* noted, "Miss Weber's plays are always thoughtful and thought-compelling, deeply understanding of human nature and soul-searching in their revelation of truth." The best of the extant early Rex dramas written and directed by Weber is *Suspense*, released on July 6, 1912. Weber uses the camera in both an objective and subjective fashion as she tells of a tramp's breaking into the isolated home of a woman while her husband races to the rescue. Weber adopts a triple screen technique to show the wife telephoning her husband as the tramp begins his invasion of their property.

Admired and respected by Carl Laemmle, Lois Weber was also much liked by her fellow workers at Universal. In 1913, she was elected mayor of Universal City, serving alongside Chief of Police Stella Adams (a comedienne with the Nestor Comedy Company) and Fire Chief Laura Oakley (a buxom character actress). She ran on the suffragist (*sic*) ticket, and when asked as to her political agenda, she replied, "I cannot go into detail, but I can say that cleanliness in municipal rule and cleanliness in picture making will be the basis of my endeavors."

In a surprise move, in June 1914, Weber and Smalley left Universal to join Bosworth, Inc., founded by actor Hobart Bosworth. Here, they directed six feature films—*The Hypocrites* (1914), *False Colors* (1914), *It's No Laughing Matter* (1914), *Sunshine Molly* (1915), *Captain Courtesy* (1915), and *Betty in Search of a Thrill* (1915) —and one short subject, *The Traitors* (1914). The last was the first film on which Frances Marion worked as an actress and an assistant to Weber.

In the spring on 1915, the couple returned to Universal, where they were to remain until 1917. Here, she directed some sixteen feature films and a handful of short subjects. Aside from the controversial film subjects, Weber directed Anna Pavlova in her first and only feature film appearance, *The Dumb Girl of Portici* (1916), and discovered actress Mary MacLaren. MacLaren was the first of a group of major silent stars discovered by Weber, in whose number are Priscilla Dean, Esther Ralston, Mildred Harris, and Billie Dove.

On March 24, 1917, *Motion Picture News* announced that Lois Weber had formed her own independent company, Lois Weber Productions, and had established her own studio at a large, Southern-style mansion at 4634 Santa

Monica Boulevard in Hollywood. The small size of the new facility determined the type of productions that Weber was to make in the future. Epics such as *The Dumb Girl of Portici* would be impossible to stage, and instead Weber decided to concentrate on domestic dramas, often dealing with the interrelationships between husbands and wives. The first seven films that Weber produced at her own studio featured Mildred Harris, whose 1918 marriage to Charlie Chaplin overshadowed her credibility as an actress. When Mildred Harris was signed to a contract by Louis B. Mayer, Weber discovered a new leading lady in Claire Windsor, who starred for the director in five independent features: *To Please One Woman* (1920), *What's Worth While* (1921), *Too Wise Wives* (1921), *The Blot* (1921), and *What Do Men Want?* (1921).

The Blot is the best of the group, notable for a careful attention to detail and the building of the characters as Weber compares the college professor's family with the "foreign-born" shoemaker, his wife, and children next door. There is something of a fixation with shoes, with which Weber appears to have been obsessed since making *Shoes* (1916), in which Mary MacLaren played an impoverished store clerk who sold her body for the price of new footwear. Claire Windsor was a major discovery in that she underplays almost consistently, while her leading man, Louis Calhern, is above reproach.

In 1921, the lease expired on the Santa Monica Boulevard property, and that coupled with relatively unenthusiastic reviews for her own films led her to give up her independence. She was also fighting—in vain—to save her marriage.

In 1923, she returned to Universal to direct *A Chapter in Her Life*, which is nothing more than a program picture but one which has great charm as a young girl, aided by the writings of Mary Baker Eddy, spreads a little happiness through her grandfather's household. Following completion of the production, Weber entered the bleakest period in her life. She lost faith in her career, locked herself away in her home, and even possibly contemplated suicide. She was saved by Captain Harry Gantz, something of an opportunist, who persuaded Weber to marry him—and coincidentally let him manage her considerable fortune. Adela Rogers St. Johns told me that Weber never seemed very dynamic, but with Gantz at her side—at home but not at the studio—Weber was able to revive her career.

Universal asked her to return to direct two features, *The Marriage Clause* (1926) and *Sensation Seekers* (1927), both starring Billie Dove. When the Universal contract came up for renewal, Weber decided to move to United Artists, where she was to direct the Duncan Sisters in the screen adaptation of their popular musical comedy success, *Topsy and Eva*. Unfortunately, Weber and the Duncan Sisters did not see eye to eye, particularly with regard to the strong racist quality of the production, and Weber departed. In 1927, she was hired by Cecil B. DeMille to direct *The Angel of Broadway*, starring two of his contract players, Leatrice Joy and Victor Varconi. For Weber, it was an interesting film dealing with a nightclub entertainer who attends a Salvation Army meeting and is recruited to the cause.

The coming of sound presented problems for Weber as it did for many male pioneering directors. For a while, she became involved in promoting the motion picture as an educational tool, writing but never filming a number of scenarios. Her interest in visual education dates back at least to 1916, and in 1925-1926, she had worked with Carl Laemmle in trying to inaugurate a system of visual education in schools.

Again, and for a last time, it was Carl Laemmle who came to Weber's aid, inviting her to return to Universal to write and direct a film based on a short story, "Glamour," by Edna Ferber. Despite producing three screenplays and reaching the stage of casting Doris Kenyon as her leading lady, Weber was abruptly pulled from the project. *Glamour* was eventually released in April 1934, starring Constance Cummings and directed by William Wyler.

From Universal it was a long way down to Seven Seas Corporation and Pinnacle Productions, for whom Lois Weber directed her last, and only sound film, *White Heat*, in the fall of 1933. A melodrama shot on location in Hawaii, *White Heat* generated little interest and was described by Andre Sennwald in the *New York Times* (June 16, 1934) as "A humorless account of the amorous difficulties of a young sugar planter." Lois Weber never lost heart. She continued to write on a speculative basis, and as late as 1939, she submitted an idea to Cecil B. DeMille. She died at the good Samaritan Hospital in Los Angeles on November 13, 1939, with her best friend, Frances Marion, at her side. It is said that Marion paid for Weber's funeral, although there is no documentation as to this or any evidence that Weber was penniless in her last years.

Lois Weber's contribution to the film industry is considerable. She was as fine a scriptwriter as she was a director, and the intelligence of her writings for the screen demonstrate an intellect that might equally have been active in the literary scene. If anything, Weber's scripts are too academic. There are moments when she forgets that a film must entertain and begins to lecture on ideas or movements that interest her. For example, in *The Hand That Rocks the Cradle*, she devoted three lengthy titles, one after the other, to pointing out that because of a lack of access to birth control literature more than 100,000 abortions are performed annually in the United States. One simple title, "If the lawmakers had to bear children, they would change the laws," says it all far more succinctly and entertainingly. Similarly, in *The Blot*, the Louis Calhern character quotes at length from *Literary Digest,* when the editorial comment in the publication has already been firmly endorsed by the story up to that point.

The scripts are as important to a Lois Weber production as the direction. Weber understood this, and, in a way, she was more interested in the storylines than in the technical aspects of filmmaking. But she understood and was familiar with both. As she said back in 1916:

> A real director should be absolute. He alone knows the effects he wants to produce, and he alone should have authority in the arrangement, cutting, titling or anything else which it may be found necessary to do to the finished product. What other artist has his creative work interfered with by someone else?...We ought to realize that the work of a picture director, worthy of the name, is creative. The purely mechanical side of producing interests me. The camera is fascinating to me. I long for stereoscopic and natural color photography, but I would sacrifice the latter for the former.[4]

Lois Weber had tremendous influence on other women directors. Lule Warrenton, Elsie Jane Wilson, Cleo Madison, Jeanie MacPherson, and Frances Marion all worked with her at the beginnings of their careers. Two male directors, Rupert Julian and Frank Lloyd, began their careers with Weber. And two of the great and highly regarded directors of American cinema began their careers as prop boys for Lois Weber. Until his death in 1985, Henry Hathaway always spoke with affection of Weber and of his debt to her. John Ford never mentioned the Weber connection, and none of the countless writers who have glorified his career have chosen to note the Lois Weber relationship.

The failure of those involved in the women's movement and in women's studies to discuss the work of Lois Weber is equally tragic. While Dorothy Arzner, in large part because she was a lesbian, is elevated to a plateau on which can be found the leading figures of the American cinema, Lois Weber remains a shadowy figure, unsung and unrecognized because she needed a man at her side and because, while she took a courageous stand on the issue of birth control, she was adamant in her opposition to abortion.

History has not been very nice to Lois Weber. It is little wonder that, when asked in 1927 what she would say to women who wanted to be directors, she replied, "Don't try it."[5] Lois Weber was a preacher whose pulpit was the motion picture. She presented her point of view in highly commercial and successful productions for Universal, and she was as much a central figure in that studio's success as was its founder, Carl Laemmle. Indeed, Carl Laemmle's tribute to her might well serve as her epitaph:

I would trust Miss Weber with any sum of money that she needed to make any picture that she wanted to make. I would be sure that she would bring it back. She knows the Motion Picture business as few people do and can drive herself as hard as anyone I have ever known.[6]

Notes

1. Quoted in Aline Carter, "The Muse of the Reel," *Motion Picture Magazine*, vol. XXI, no. 2, March 1921, p. 62.

2. Quoted in *The Moving Picture World*, vol. XVII, no. 6, August 9, 1913, p. 640.

3. Lois Weber, "How I Became a Motion Picture Director," *Static Flashes*, vol. 1, no. 14, April 24, 1915, p. 8.

4. Quoted in Mlle. Chic, "The Greatest Woman Director in the World," *The Moving Picture Weekly*, vol. II, no. 21, May 20, 1916, p. 25.

5. Quoted in Charles S. Dunning, "The Gate Women Don't Crash," *Liberty*, vol. IV, no. 2, May 14, 1927, p. 33.

6. Quoted in Winifred Aydelotte, "The Little Red Schoolhouse Becomes a Theatre," *Motion Picture Magazine*, vol. XLVII, no. 2, March 1934, p. 85.

Chapter Four

The Universal Women

The largest aggregation of women directors at one studio during the silent era was to be found at Universal. Most other producers employed one, or perhaps two women directors at most. Universal at one point in the teens had as many as nine under contract. Lois Weber was the most prominent, but the others produced films that were highly regarded in their day and enjoyed careers as directors lasting through several films and sometimes several years.

In his legendary biography of Carl Laemmle, the founder of Universal Pictures, British author John Drinkwater wrote, "Laemmle also startled the trade by giving women commissions to direct his pictures. Lois Weber, the most famous of them, Ida May Park, and Cleo Madison, were among the pioneers of his revolutionary suffrage."[1] It is doubtful that Laemmle's concern for women's rights had much, if anything, to do with his hiring of women as directors. Rather, his studio embarked on a heavy production and release schedule, and having committed itself to a certain number of films a year, Universal found it had an insufficient number of directors under contract. Rather than hire additional directors from outside, at heavy expense, it was far simpler and economically sound to find such directors in the ranks of the studio's contract actors, screenwriters, and editors—and among these groups were large numbers of women.

John Drinkwater describes Carl Laemmle variously as "a clear sighted pioneer...a good man" and "a remarkable man."[2] Such statements are certainly justified both in terms of Laemmle's extraordinary vision in building one of the few studios in Los Angeles that has survived in size and strength to the present and in regard to his ability to recognize talented women among his staff. Universal's founder is often referred to as Uncle Carl, indicative of the feeling around his studio that the employees were one big happy family—not to mention Laemmle's fondness for nepotism in his hiring practices—and in the Universal family of the teens, the female directors were the matriarchal figures, well-liked and respected by their colleagues. As Universal leading lady Ruth Clifford recalled,

> When the women directed the films, the other directors, the men, were very cooperative. And the actors didn't resent it at all because a woman was directing. They took direction just the same as if it were a man directing. Everyone cooperated. It was like a big happy family at that studio—the same players were there, the same directors, and the same women directors.

The most prominent actress at Universal to become a director was Cleo Madison. Born in 1883 and educated in Bloomington, Illinois, Madison had an extensive career on the stage and in vaudeville before joining Universal. She was director Rex Ingram's leading lady in two of his early feature films, *The Chalice of Sorrow* (1916) and *Black Orchids* (1917). Madison began directing late in 1915, handling both two-reel dramatic shorts and features. She claimed to have gained her first directorial assignment by the simple expedient of rejecting all the male directors she was to work for. "I had seen men with less brains than I have getting away with it, and so I knew that I could direct if they'd give me the opportunity," she told *Photoplay*.[3]

The fan magazine also reported that Madison was as difficult, if necessary, as any of her male counterparts. An assistant cameraman was reported to have said, "You ought to see 'em hop when they do what she don't want 'em to! There ain't a director on the lot that's got the flow of language or can exhibit the temperament she can when she gets good an' peeved."[4]

Cleo Madison directed and starred in two five-reel features for Universal. The first, *A Soul Enslaved*, was released on January 24, 1916. Very much a woman's picture in that the original story was by a woman, Adele Farrington, and a prominent female screenwriter, Olga Printzlau, adapted it, *A Soul Enslaved* featured Madison as an activist fighting for better working conditions for her fellow factory employees. According to *The Moving Picture World* (January 15, 1916), "This five reel production goes deeply into the more vital problems of human relationship, picturing the manner in which two people who have transgressed finally find happiness in each other's love." In *Motion Picture News* (January 22, 1916), Peter Milne described *A Soul Enslaved* as "a picture based on 'the woman with a past' theme, done in a highly satisfying and convincing way."

The second feature, *Her Bitter Cup*, released on April 17, 1916, also has Madison as a factory worker, but here the similarity with *A Soul Enslaved* ends. According to *The Moving Picture World* (April 22, 1916), Madison played Rethna,

> a girl raised in a sordid slum district. She nurses the sick and even steals for them. Later the elder son of the factory owner fancies her and fits her up in an

apartment. The contrasts of life are pleasing here, but the relations of the girl with Harry Burke are not made clear. In fact, at this point a number of mixed motives and obscurities creep into the story. The crucifixion of the girl's body at the close seems revolting. The story is quite strong in some respects, but certain features seem to lack proper significance.

In *Motion Picture News* (April 8, 1916), Peter Milne wrote that Madison's "acting is emotional and strong and her work as a director is good. The settings and the light effects deserve unusual commendation." But, ultimately, Milne concluded, "the full possibilities of this picture have not been realized."

Among the two-reel shorts that Madison directed and also starred in, during 1916, are *Eleanor's Catch, Alias Jane Jones, The Guilty One* (co-directed with William V. Mong), *The Girl in Lower 9* (co-directed with William V. Mong), *Priscilla's Prisoner,* and *When the Wolf Howls.* The only film directed by Madison known to exist is *Her Defiance,* a two-reel Rex drama, co-directed by Joe King and released on January 14, 1916. Madison stars as a woman supposedly deserted by her wealthy young lover. After giving birth to his son, she meets up with him again as a cleaning woman in his office. For the first time, the man discovers that he has a child and that his father broke up the relationship. *Her Defiance* is a powerful melodrama, making good use of the matte process as the two leads explain at their reunion what each thought had transpired. "A sympathetic subject along conventional lines but benefited by several original situations that add much to its value" was the opinion of *Motion Picture News* (January 15, 1916).

Cleo Madison's character in *Her Defiance* is a strong one, but generally she was cast as simpering heroines, far removed from the militancy that the actress displayed in real life. As *Photoplay*'s William M. Henry reported,

> Cleo Madison is a womanly woman—if she were otherwise she couldn't play sympathetic parts as she does—and yet she is so smart and businesslike that she makes most of the male population of Universal City look like debutantes when it comes right down to brass tacks and affairs.
>
> "One of these days men are going to get over the fool idea that women have no brains," she told me, "and quit getting insulted at the thought that a skirt-wearer can do their work quite as well as they can. And I don't believe that day is very far distant, either." You have to converse with Cleo Madison to get the correct impression of her. To see her in pictures tells you absolutely nothing of her real character.[5]

Cleo Madison's time as a director was all too short, as were her years as a star. By the 1920s, she was playing minor roles in minor films. In later years, she recalled for one of her fans, "I went into 'white collar' work about 1931 and am retired now. Just growing old. I am sending you several of my remnants of old pictures. Keep what you like and dispose of the rest as I have no need of them. The Silent Film! Those were the happy days." Cleo Madison died, alone and forgotten, in Burbank, California, on March 11, 1964.

Ruth Stonehouse was born in Denver, Colorado, on September 28, 1892, and came to fame as an actress at Essanay, usually playing opposite Bryant Washburn. She came to Universal in 1916 and was usually teamed with leading man Jack Mulhall. She had a number of strong roles on screen, including a female detective in *Kinkaid, Gambler* (1916) and a prima ballerina in *Love Never Dies* (1916), and *In Love Aflame* (1917) she travels from the United States to Constantinople, disguised as a man.

As far as can be ascertained, Stonehouse began directing in the spring of 1917, and one of her first films, in which she also starred, was the two-reel Victor comedy, *Dorothy Dares*. According to *Moving Picture Stories* (April 13, 1917), Stonehouse was never happier than when she was playing child roles and "experiencing the feelings of a little girl again." Such was Universal's excuse for her directing and starring in a series of Mary Ann Kelly stories. She was certainly petite, leading a contemporary writer to comment, "It seems incredible that this delicate, dainty little creature could be so masterful as to dominate a band of fiery photoplayers."

Like Cleo Madison, Ruth Stonehouse's years as a star were over by 1920. She played second leads and then character parts with the coming of sound. Stonehouse died in Los Angeles on May 12, 1941.

In 1913 Lule Warrenton joined Universal as an actress specializing in mother roles. She made her feature film debut with Cleo Madison in the Biblical drama, *Samson* (1914). Born in Flint, Michigan, on June 22, 1862, by the time, she joined Universal, Lule Warrenton was a buxom, middle-aged woman who had been on the stage virtually all her life. In 1916, at the suggestion of one of its male directors, Otis Turner, Universal decided to have Mrs. Warrenton direct a series of children's shorts, featuring child actresses Clara Horton and a black youngster, Ernestine Jones; the first of such shorts was titled *The Calling of Lindy*. As was customary at Universal, Mrs. Warrenton had her own company, consisting of Allan Watt as her assistant director, and Nora Dempsey, Irma Sorter, and Benjamin Suslow as supporting players.

Early in 1917, the actress left Universal to form her own company, the Frieder Film Corporation, with studios at Lankershim, California. As *The Moving Picture World* (February 17, 1917) explained,

> The big idea "Mother" Warrenton has had ever since she quit directing pictures for Universal is to produce photoplays with children as actors for the most part, the plays to present the comedies and the tragedies and the dramas of child-life, just as they appear to the child mind. She has studied the proposition deeply, and believes that by writing her own scenes and supervising the entire production, she can produce photoplays that will be intensely interesting to both old and young, and entirely suitable for children.

The Frieder Film Corporation's first and only feature, written and directed by Mrs. Warrenton, was *A Bit o' Heaven*, adapted from the popular children's tale, *The Bird's Christmas Carol*, by Kate Douglas Wiggin. It told the story of a poor family of eight children, the "Raggedy Ruggleses," who are invited for Christmas dinner to the mansion of a wealthy family, whose only child is a little crippled girl. *A Bit o' Heaven* was well received by the trade press. *Exhibitor's Trade Review* (June 23, 1917) described it as "an unusually high-class production filled with charming originality....While the theme is simple and devoid of complexities of plot, it has all the appealing charm of youthful pathos." In *Motion Picture News* (July 7, 1917), William J. McGrath described the film as "something new and refreshing, a new defense of motion pictures."

Despite the success of *A Bit o' Heaven*, the Frieder Film Corporation produced no further films. Two further productions, *The Littlest Fugitive* and *Hop o' My Thumb*, were announced, but there is no evidence that they were ever made. The company disappeared, and in September 1917, Lule Warrenton was back at Universal—as an actress. Her career there as an actress is not without interest in that she played leading character roles in four features directed by women. Warrenton appeared in both of Cleo Madison's features; she was in Elsie Jane Wilson's *The Silent Lady* (1917), and played the housekeeper, Mrs. Forbes, in Lois Weber's *Jewel*.

Lule Warrenton continued to act until 1922, when she announced her retirement. For a middle-aged woman, she had enjoyed a strenuous career in the film industry, not only as an actress and director, but also as founder of the Hollywood Girls' Club. She made one last attempt to return to film direction in the summer of 1923, when she formed what was billed as "the first all-woman film company," headed by herself, assisted by Mrs. A. B. E. Shute, Mrs. Katherine Chesnaye, and Miss Edith Kendall. *Camera!* (June 23, 1923) reported that "Its first production has been made, and preparations are on the way for making a large regular program of feature releases, educationals, and other films in San Diego at the Sawyer-Lubin Studios." Nothing came of the venture, but Mrs. Warrenton remained in the San Diego area, retiring to her avocado ranch near Carlsbad, where she died on May 14, 1932. Her son, Gilbert Warrenton, became a prominent cinematographer.

Grace Cunard and Francis Ford (brother of director John) were a popular starring team in Universal serials of the teens, their most famous being *The Broken Coin*, released in 1915. Aside from starring in the serials. Cunard also wrote and occasionally directed episodes. With Ford, she wrote, directed, and starred in a handful of short subjects, including *Lady Raffles Returns* (1916), *Born of the People* (1916) and *The Terrors of War* (1917). The first is of more than passing interest in that it is a feminist detective drama. In 1914, Cunard directed a burlesque of the Civil War, titled *Sheridan's Pride*, released on March 4 and featuring Ernie Shields as General Philip Sheridan. Born in Columbus, Ohio, on April 8, 1893, Grace Cunard died at the Motion Picture Country House in Woodland Hills, California, on August 9, 1978. She was still remembered with affection by serial buffs, but her work as a director was long forgotten.

Elsie Jane Wilson directed some ten feature films at Universal during 1917 and 1918, yet she remains forgotten not only as a director but also an actress, while her husband, Rupert Julian, though not exactly a major figure in film history, still warrants passing attention. Born in New Zealand on November 7, 1890, Elsie Jane Wilson began her acting career at the age of two. With Rupert Julian, she came to the United States around 1913, and the two appeared on the legitimate stage until joining Universal's Rex Company in the summer of 1914, working as actors under the direction of Joseph de Grasse. Wilson left Universal briefly in 1915 and 1916, appearing in feature films for other companies, including *The Lure of the Mask* (1915) for American; and *Temptation* (1915) and *Oliver Twist* (1916, as Nancy Sikes) for Jesse L. Lasky. At Universal, Wilson generally appeared in films directed by her husband, including *Bettina Loved a Soldier* (1916), *The Evil Women Do* (1916), *A Kentucky Cinderella* (1917), *The Circus of Life* (1917) and *Mother o' Mine* (1917).

While starring for her husband, Elsie Jane Wilson also began to assist in the direction and later to co-direct. "We like the same kind of pictures," she told *Photoplay*, "but we have such different ideas of how to get the same effects that if we ever talked over our work we'd fight all the time."[6]

Elsie Jane Wilson began her solo directorial career in 1917 with four features starring child actress Zoe Ray, who was billed as "The Universal Baby." The first, *The Little Pirate*, released on September 10, 1917, had Ray involved with a group of juvenile pirates. It was followed by *The Silent Lady*, *The Cricket*, and *My Little Boy*. *The Cricket* told the story of an orphan child adopted by three old actors, and was praised as "a most satisfactory production" by Peter Milne in *Motion Picture News* (November 24, 1917). But on the whole, critical response to the Zoe Ray features was poor. *The New York Dramatic Mirror* (December 15, 1917) opined that *My Little Boy* "should recommend itself to audiences comprised for the most part of women and children. What parts of it aren't dull are insipid." "A cheap feature at best" was *Variety*'s (November 23, 1917) opinion of *The Silent Lady*.

Carmel Myers was the star of Elsie Jane Wilson's 1918 features *The City of Tears* and *The Dream Lady*. Of the latter, Peter Milne wrote in *Motion Picture News* (July 6, 1918),

> There is not very much of plot material to this five-reeler, but what there is is handled nicely and will prove a winner. Pathos and humaneness are the dominant features, and these always find a ready appeal...The whole cast is well selected, the locations fairly well selected and the direction is moderately good.

In the same year, Ella Hall was the star of *Beauty in Chains* and *New Love for Old*, and interestingly and very unusually for a Universal feature, the latter was billed as an Ella Hall Production.

Alice Guy Blaché

Alice Guy Blaché with Yvonne and Germaine Serand, the players in her first film, *La Feé aux Choux* (1896).

La Vie du Christ (1906), directed by Alice Guy Blaché.

Lois Weber leading her army of male workers.

The Hypocrites (1914), directed by Lois Weber; the woman is Jane Darwell.

MOTION PICTURE NEWS   Vol. XIV. No. 16. Section 2

MR. AND MRS. JOSEPH DeGRASSE

JOSEPH DeGRASSE
Director

Now Producing
" The Price of Silence "

In Preparation
" The Piper's Price "

Now on

THEIR 78th RELEASE

with the

UNIVERSAL FILM MFG.

CO.

making

" FEATURES "

IDA MAY PARK
(Mrs. Joseph DeGrasse)
Writer and Adapter
Latest Features:
" Father and the Boys "
" The Grip of Jealousy "
" Tangled Hearts "
" The Gilded Spider "
" If My Country Should Call "
" The Place Beyond the Winds "
" The Price of Silence "
" The Piper's Price "

CONTRACT UNIVERSAL FILM CO. EXPIRES JAN. 1st, 1917.

Lule Warrenton

Cleo Madison

Jeanie MacPherson

A scene from *The Devil's Prize* (1916), directed by Marguerite Bertsch.

Frances Marion

Ruth Clifford, who was a close friend of both Elsie Jane Wilson and Rupert Julian, starred in Wilson's *The Lure of Luxury*, released on October 7, 1918, and *The Game's Up*, released on January 20, 1919. The former was praised by P. S. Harrison in *Motion Picture News* (September 28, 1918) for the emotionalism of Clifford's performance. *The Game's Up* was a farce, with Clifford's pretending to a friend that she is a wealthy woman with an automobile, and co-starred Charles Ray's brother, Al. "Simply a scream" opined P. S. Harrison in *Motion Picture News* (January 18, 1919).

The Game's Up marked the end of Elsie Jane Wilson's career. "Is directing a man's work—I should say it is!" she told *Photoplay*.[7] Her husband continued as a prominent director through the end of the silent era, taking over the direction of *Merry-Go-Round* from Erich von Stroheim in 1923 and directing Lon Chaney in *The Phantom of the Opera* in 1925. As an actor, Julian became well known for his impersonation of the German Kaiser, most notably in *The Kaiser, the Beast of Berlin* (1918). He died in 1943, and Elsie Jane Wilson died in Los Angeles on January 16, 1965.

After an early career in newspaper and publicity work, Connecticut-born Ruth Ann Baldwin joined Universal as a writer. One of her first major assignments was the script for the 1915 Herbert Rawlinson-Anna Little serial, *The Black Box*, and in connection therewith, Baldwin had been sent to London for six months by Carl Laemmle to collaborate with novelist E. Phillips Oppenheim. In 1916, Baldwin assisted Lynn Reynolds with the direction of *End of the Rainbow*, featuring Myrtle Gonzalez. Her first film as a solo director was *The Mother Call*, a one-reel drama, starring Dorothy Davenport, released on November 30, 1916. Prior to promotion to director, according to *Motion Picture News* (March 17, 1917), Baldwin had served as "film critic and editor" at Universal. *Photoplay* (October 1916) noted, "She has long been regarded as one of the most capable of Universal's staff."

Ruth Ann Baldwin directed two feature films at Universal. The first, *A Wife on Trial*, released on July 30, 1917, was written by and starred Leo O. Pierson (whom Baldwin had married on February 17, 1917). The story concerned a woman (Mignon Anderson) whose husband overcomes his psychosomatic paralysis and defends her when she is attacked by a burglar.

The second Baldwin feature is important not only because it survives but also because it is a Western, indicative of the potential women had for directing any genre in the teens. *'49-'17*, released on October 15, 1917, was also written by Baldwin, based on an *Argosy* magazine short story, and again starred Leo O. Pierson. Its story involves a judge who took part in the 1849 gold rush and wants to relive those days through the recreation of a mining camp, peopled with members of a theatrical troupe. Play acting becomes reality when the judge's male secretary falls in love with the daughter of the owner of the general store and is kidnapped by a professional gambler (played by Jean Hersholt). Gold is actually discovered close to the town, and the gambler stages a real holdup

Filmed on location near San Diego, *'49-'17* was well liked by the trade paper reviewers. In *Motion Picture News* (October 27, 1917), Peter Milne wrote,

> This type of plot extends many possibilities, both of a humorous and a dramatic order to the picture producer, and Universal has chosen to place almost entire stress upon the latter element. The results are satisfactory though it must be confessed the introduction offered such a rosy prospect that they fail to come up to expectations in every department. The scenes

seem to lack a certain snap and sustaining power that, if present, would have welded them into a much more powerful whole. Even as it is, however, '49-'17 offers entertainment consistent with its companion Butterflies [Butterfly was the brand name under which the film was produced by Universal] and there are places where the originality of the idea carries it to stronger heights.

Motography (October 27, 1917) commented,

The direction should be well complimented as to the thrilling climax. There is no doubt in this case that the director had a good story to work with, especially during the escape and capture of a gambler, but still the keen foresight of the producer presented the finale in a way that at least overcame to a slight degree the laggy moments occurring during the second and third acts. Many of the exterior locations have been well selected, and the Western atmosphere has been ably maintained throughout, adding a tinge of realism to the release in its entirety. The photography is also worthy of praise.

It would be foolish to pretend that '49-'17 is a great silent Western, but it does boast an original story that is well handled both in the script and the direction. There is no great acting—or great actors for that matter—apparent on screen, but there is considerable enthusiasm that overcomes the shortcomings of some of the performances. In all, '49-'17 proves that women were more than capable of directing "B" Westerns that could stand as equal to any directed by their male counterparts, and, quite frankly, '49-'17 is more entertaining and more inceptive than most

"B" Westerns turned out by Hollywood in the 1930s and 1940s.

In 1919, Ruth Ann Baldwin returned to screenwriting, and her last credits were in 1921. What happened to her later is unknown. When Leo O. Pierson died in 1943, Ruth Ann Baldwin was not his wife. The couple had either divorced or she had predeceased him.

Jeanie MacPherson is well remembered for her work as a scenarist for Cecil B. DeMille. Among the major scripts she wrote or co-wrote for the director in the teens are *The Cheat* (1915), starring Sessue Hayakawa and Fannie Ward, *Joan the Woman* (1916), starring Geraldine Farrar, *The Little American* (1917), starring Mary Pickford, and *Male and Female* (1919), starring Gloria Swanson. Prior to joining DeMille at the Jesse L. Lasky Feature Play Company in 1914, MacPherson had been under contract to Universal as an actress. She appeared in *The Merchant of Venice* (1914), directed by Lois Weber and Phillips Smalley, worked as a scenario writer for Universal, and also became a director of its short subjects released under the Powers brand name.

As she recalled in a 1916 interview, Jeanie MacPherson had written the script for a one-reel drama, *The Tarantula*, in which she also starred as a mining camp follower known as the Tarantula, who, perhaps not surprisingly, dies from a a tarantula bite.[8] Edwin August was the initial director, but after he left Universal, the negative of the film was accidentally destroyed, and MacPherson was asked to remake it, handling the directorial chores. "The story is not strong, although there is a moment of suspense when she discovers the spider on her breast," commented *The Moving Picture World* (May 10, 1913).

As reported at the time, the amount of work required of her at Universal, directing, writing, and starring in Powers brand dramas led to "nervous prostration." Jeanie MacPherson met Cecil B. DeMille, and he persuaded her to quit Universal. She devoted the rest of her life to the producer-director and was for a time his mistress. Born in Boston on May 18, 1887, Jeanie MacPherson had begun her screen career as an actress with the American Biograph Company in 1908, later moving to Edison prior to joining Universal. She died in Hollywood on August 26, 1946.

After Lois Weber, the most important of the Universal women directors is Ida May Park. Aside from Weber and Alice Guy Blaché, she is the only one to have spoken and written at length on the subject of women as directors. On the set, Ida May Park was a hard taskmistress. One of her leading ladies, Mary MacLaren, who also worked for Lois Weber, recalled that Park was known around the studio as Mrs. Simon Legree: "She was certainly a terrible, terrible slave driver."[9] Some of that quality, that strength and determination, is apparent in what Ida May Park told interviewers at the time.

In a 1918 interview with *Photoplay*, she commented,

> It was because directing seemed so utterly unsuited to a woman that I refused the first company offered me. I don't know why I looked at it that way, either. A woman can bring to this work splendid enthusiasm and imagination; a natural love of detail and an intuitive knowledge of character. All of these are supposed to be feminine traits, and yet they are all necessary to the successful director. Of course, in order to put on a picture, a woman must have broadness of viewpoint, a sense of humor, and firmness of character—there are times when every director must be something of a martinet—but these characteristics are necessary to balance the others.

It has been said that a woman worries over, loves, and works for, her convictions exactly as though they were her children. Consequently, her greatest danger is in taking them and herself too seriously.

Directing is a recreation to me, and I want my people to do good work because of their regard for me and not because I browbeat them into it....I believe in choosing distinct types and then seeing that the actor puts his own personality into his parts, instead of making every part in a picture reflect my personality.[10]

Two years later, Ida May Park returned to the topic in the trade paper, *Camera!*

Why shouldn't a woman engage in this work? She is more imaginative, more romantic and more spiritual. Woman leads in story writing today, as the magazine pages testify. If she has thus proven her superiority at creating characters and situations, why should it not be so in transcribing them to the screen? If this fitness is conceded and the objections are technical, what are they?

One thing weighs heavily in our favor. Films are made for women; they compose the large majority of the fans and it is proverbial among producers that you must first please their sex in the making of pictures. This being so it follows that a member of the sex is best able to gauge their wants in the form of stories and plays. In staging scenes of romance, for example, who knows as well as a woman what will ring true for her sisters in the theatre?

So if the picture play is purely a selling proposition, the argument is on the side of my sex. As for the technical considerations, it is true that directing is

largely a matter of leadership. On that score I have
never had the slightest trouble. Here again the tact of
woman comes to her aid and she may get results from
her players that male directors get from severer methods, and so I have found it.[11]

Born in Los Angeles on December 28, 1879, Ida May
Park went on the stage at the age of fifteen. It was in the
theater that she met her husband, fellow actor Joseph de
Grasse. When the latter joined Pathé as an actor, in 1909,
his wife also entered films as a scenario writer. The couple
joined Universal, and Park's first credits as a screenwriter
appear on Rex and Nestor brand films of 1914. She was a
prolific scenario writer of films directed by her husband,
and the couple worked as a production team. Their first
feature for Universal was *Father and the Boys* (1915).

In 1917, Ida May Park began her career as a solo director,
with her first production being *The Flashlight*, released on
May 21 and starring Dorothy Phillips. In all, Park directed
some fourteen films, the majority of which starred
Dorothy Phillips, Universal's major dramatic star of the
period. For Phillips, Ida May Park supplied the scripts for
If My Country Should Call (1916), *The Place Beyond the Winds*
(1916), *The Price of Silence* (1916), *The Piper's Price* (1917),
Hell Morgan's Girl (1917), *The Girl in the Checkered Coat*
(1917), and *A Dolls' House* (1917). She directed and wrote
the scripts for the following Dorothy Phillips vehicles: *The
Flashlight* (1917), *Fires of Rebellion* (1917), *The Rescue* (1917),
Bondage (1917), *Broadway Love* (1918), *The Grand Passion*
(1918), and *The Risky Road* (1918).

In 1920, Ida May Park and her husband left Universal.
Park's last three films as a director were for independent
companies. For Louis Gasnier, she directed *The Butterfly
Man*, released on April 18, 1920, starring Lew Cody. Park's
last two films were co-directed with her husband, both

made for Andrew J. Callaghan Productions, and both starred Bessie Love: *Bonnie May*, released in October 1920, and *The Midlanders*, released in December 1920.

For reasons unknown, Ida May Park disappeared from the directing scene in 1920. Joseph de Grasse continued to direct through the 1920s and in 1926, his wife contributed the script to his feature, *The Hidden Way*. Ida May Park died in Los Angeles County on June 13, 1954.

In 1920, the Boston publishing house of Houghton Mifflin published *Careers for Women*, edited by Catherine Filene. *The New York Times* (December 26, 1920) praised the work, noting, "Differently as the various authors write, there is uniformity in one respect—in the brisk, snappy, pungent way in which they push their points at you and make you see the picture." Intended to provide vocational information to high school and college women, the subjects covered by *Careers for Women* included advertising, architecture, business, health services, library work, physical education, secretarial work—and motion pictures! Writing on a potential career for women as a film director was Ida May Park. It speaks volumes that when *Careers for Women* was reprinted by Houghton Mifflin in a "revised and enlarged" edition in 1934, the chapter on film directing was conspicuously absent.

Notes

1. John Drinkwater, *The Life and Adventures of Carl Laemmle*, London: William Heinemann, 1931, p. 195.

2. Ibid, p. 275 and p. 1, respectively.

3. William M. Henry, "Cleo, the Craftswoman," *Photoplay*, vol. IX, no. 2, January 1916, p. 111.

4. Ibid., p. 111.

5. Ibid., p. 109.

6. Frances Denton, "Lights! Camera! Quiet!" *Photoplay*, vol. XIII, no. 3, February 1918, p. 50.

7. Ibid.

8. This story is recounted in Alice Martin, "From 'Wop' Parts to Bossing the Job," *Photoplay*, vol. X, no. 5, October 1916, pp. 95-97. In this article, MacPherson claims that *The Tarantula* was "the most popular and profitable film the company has produced," but this seems rather unlikely.

9. Quoted in Richard Koszarski, "Truth or Reality?: A Few Thoughts on Mary MacLaren's Shoes," *Griffithiana*, no. 40/42, October 1991, p. 82.

10. Quoted in Frances Denton, "Lights! Camera! Quiet!" *Photoplay*, vol. XIII, no. 3, February 1918, p. 49.

11. "Women Best Fitted To Direct Pictures, Says One of Them," *Camera!* vol. II, no. 39, January 10, 1920, p. 8.

Chapter Five

Vitagraph's Women Directors

Founded in the 1890s by two Englishmen, J. Stuart Blackton and Albert E. Smith, the Vitagraph Company of America boasted a surprising number of female directors during its long and glorious life. In total, it could not match Universal, but it did produce at least one woman who contributed a number of major features and an actress-director largely responsible for the popularity of the domestic comedy genre in the 'teens. Vitagraph's pioneering actress, Florence Turner did just about everything else at Vitagraph, from keeping the books to making lunch for the company's owners, but she was never asked to direct there. With director Larry Trimble, she did form her own production company in the United Kingdom in 1913, and in the fall of 1919, she directed and starred in a series of one-reel comedies at Universal.

The first documented woman director at Vitagraph was actress Helen Gardner (1885-1968), who had first achieved prominence at the company with her portrayal of Becky Sharp in the 1912 three-reel version of *Vanity Fair*. Gardner worked closely with her husband, director Charles Gaskill, on the films which the couple made together at Vitagraph, and, in 1912, she became one of the first women to form her own production company. She returned to Vitagraph in 1915 and received co-credit as director on at least one film, the two-reel *The Still, Small Voice*, released on February 23, 1915. Gardner is featured in this production as a dumb girl, whose inheritance of a fortune makes her easy prey for a couple of villains, one of whom she murders while the other is tried for the crime. It is interesting to note, from a feminist viewpoint, that Gardner was generally cast in strong feminine roles, from *Cleopatra*, in 1912, through *Miss Jekyll and Madame Hyde*, in 1915.

Between 1914 and 1916, Vitagraph released fifteen half-reel actuality shorts from Scandinavia, photographed and directed by Alma Morganstern or Morganstein (the spelling of the last name varies from film to film). While nothing appears to be known of this filmmaker, the first name indicates that here was a woman, and one certainly worthy of further study.

The most important of Vitagraph's women directors was Marguerite Bertsch, who had commenced her career as a playwright prior to joining Vitagraph as a scenario writer around 1913. She was responsible for the scripts of a number of major Vitagraph productions, including *Captain Alvarez* (1914), *A Million Bid* (1914) and *My Official Wife* (1916), and by early 1916 was the head of the studio's scenario department.

She provided the following account of her involvement in screenwriting for the October 1914 issue of *Photoplay*:

> There is little to say concerning how I came to take up the writing of motion picture plays. I was always interested, both at Columbia University and elsewhere, in the writing of plays for the stage. When eighteen years old I was fortunate in attracting the attention of Mrs. W. C. de Mille, who very kindly offered to help me to develop what she felt to be a promising talent in this line.

While studying at college I became interested in the photoplay field, and after writing several acceptable scenarios, I became a member of the staff of the Vitagraph Company. After all, it is not so much how one happened to enter a field, as how he or she progresses, having once entered. I believe one's work should speak for one, and if it cannot do that, the less said, the better.

I have always found that a really great photoplay is great because of the self same attributes that make a great offering for the stage; wherefore the future of the silent drama is bounded like that of the stage—by the genius of those who operate in the field. That such will have a more plastic medium in the photoplay than in the stage play, and at the same time, a more rigid medium than in the novel ought to augur that the motion picture play will eventually transcend either of the other two mediums.[1]

Bertsch's first film as a director was *The Law Decides*, released on May 1, 1916, on which she worked with longtime Vitagraph director William P. S. Earle. Her first solo effort as a director was *The Devil's Prize*, a five-reel feature released on November 11, 1916. Bertsch also wrote this story of a man who blames others for his problems and later for his crimes, which co-starred Antonio Moreno and Naomi Childers. According to Ben H. Grimm in *The Moving Picture World* (November 11, 1916), "the production has considerable strength."

During 1917, Marguerite Bertsch directed two five-reel features, *The Glory of Yolande* and *The Soul Master*, as well as one short subject, *Captain Jinks and Himself*. The first, written by Maibelle Heikes Justice, starred Anita Stewart and was released on January 20, 1917. "A photoplay written by one woman, directed by another and acted by a third member of the gentler sex, should be a correct and convincing revelation of female character," commented Edward Weitzel in *The Moving Picture World* (February 3, 1917). In reality, *The Glory of Yolande* is little more than the story of an innocent Russian peasant girl who retains her innocence as she becomes a great ballerina.

The Soul Master, released on May 28, 1917, was described by Julian Johnson in *Photoplay* (August 1917) as "an uninspired photoplay, featuring Earle Williams in a heavy and apparently uncongenial role," that of a man deserted by his wife and child, and who, fifteen years later, falls in love with the latter.

Unfortunately, the films directed by Marguerite Bertsch offer little from their plot synopses and contemporary critical commentaries—the films themselves do not survive—to suggest that she was anything more than a competent, if uninspired director. There are no strong female characterizations, and the one film which does provide a major role for a female star, *The Glory of Yolande*, presents its heroine as the ultimate innocent, trading on her "purity" rather than any form of feminine strength.

Certainly, the films which Marguerite Bertsch directed were not unsuccessful, and there is no explanation as to why she chose not to continue as a director or why her career simply ends so abruptly in 1918 (a year after publication of her book, *How To Write for Moving Pictures*[2]) and she slipped into anonymity.

If Marguerite Bertsch became a director because of quantities which were proven at the studio, the same cannot be said of J. Stuart Blackton's second wife, Paula, who had definite aspirations as both a producer and director. As early as February 1915, she took over the Vitagraph Theatre at Broadway and 44th Street, New York, to present a live entertainment. *The Wood Violet* and *The Island of Regeneration* were screened in their entirety, except for their last reels, as which point the performers appeared live on stage to "pantomime" the final scenes.

Mrs. Blackton took herself very seriously indeed, and explained in the March 1917 issue of *Motion Picture Classic*:

> The time came when I realized that my very power of helping others was limited by the limitations I placed upon myself. This was particularly true of my little girl and my little boy [Violet and Charles]. I wanted to bring them up in the fullest appreciation and comprehension of their father's work. I could not do that by merely sitting in fireside sessions as privy councilor. No, no! I had surely my own personal message for pictures. I must write them—my own kind. I and our children must do them—our own kind; expressive of ourselves—therefore expressive of a million others of whom we are but the proto-types. All the mothers and all the children and all the beauty of the world seemed to call us to make pictures that should be both professional and intimate— that should embody the light and shade, and humor and pathos, which every heart knows within itself, and which may not be made to order under condi-tions ruling in a studio existing solely that stockhold-ers may draw dividends. We wanted to make pictures of ourselves in which we should be just ourselves—only a little more so![3]

The result was a series of costume films, beginning with a version of Booth Tarkington's *The Beautiful Lady*, all starring the Blackton children along with Mrs. Blackton, and directed by Mrs. Blackton at her husband's estate at Oyster Bay, Long Island. The films were financed by

J. Stuart Blackton, presumably to keep his wife happy and certainly not in any hope of financial or critical success.

After her husband had severed his ties with Vitagraph, Paula Blackton wrote and directed *The Littlest Scout*, released by Independent Sales Corporation in March 1919. The Blackton children were again featured, with Charles Stuart Blackton, wearing a Boy Scout's uniform and punching the young son of a pacifist in the nose. After being kidnapped by German spies, the two children lead the Roosevelt Boy Scout troop (named after Theodore Roosevelt who owned an estate next to Blackton's at Oyster Bay) to the Germans and help capture a submarine.

Although Sidney Drew dominates the series of domestic comedies he and his wife made, first at Vitagraph and later at Metro, from 1914 onwards, Mrs. Drew (Lucille McVey) was the creative genius behind the productions. As Sidney Drew revealed to Sue Roberts in the May 1919 issue of *Motion Picture Magazine*, Mrs. Drew wrote, directed (usually without credit), and supervised every detail of the construction of the films. "I believe she'd like to paint the furniture and make the costumes if she could,"[4] joked Drew. In the September 1917 issue of *Photoplay*, Frederick James Smith commented,

Just between ourselves, I give Mrs. Drew 75 percent of the credit for the conception of the Drew comedies. That is, she is the team member who selects an idea and builds on it. Mr. Drew has the actor's discernment to understand her mental process and to perfect it on the screen. To him goes the credit for putting the idea over.

Following the 1919 death of her husband, Mrs. Drew returned to Vitagraph in 1921, and here she directed Alice

Joyce in a five-reel feature, *Cousin Kate*, based on an early stage success of Ethel Barrymore. "Being a typically fussy masculine critic," wrote Burns Mantle in *Photoplay* (March 1921), "I naturally feel that while the dear ladies may have made the best of the material they have not made the most of it." However, Burns Mantle notwithstanding, the film was a moderate success for Vitagraph and should have— but did not—lead to Mrs. Drew's being asked to direct other features.

The problem, of course, was that women directors were making less of an impact in the twenties; their heyday had been in the teens, and only those with a major list of credits to their names, such as Lois Weber, stood much of a chance in the increasingly male-dominated industry of the new decade.

Lilian Chester suffered much as did Mrs. Sidney Drew. She had worked closely with her husband, George Randolph Chester, on many Vitagraph features from 1916 onwards but was to receive co-credit as director on only one, *The Son of Wallingford*, released on October 30, 1921. This film was an effort to garner success from the popularity of *Get-Rich-Quick Wallingford*. Chester had originally written it as a short story, and George M. Cohan had turned it into a successful play that Frank Borzage had filmed in 1921. Unfortunately the Chester film was little more than a pale imitation of the Borzage feature—"at times thrilling, at times disappointing—at all times, just a motion picture," as *Photoplay* (February 1922) commented. George Randolph Chester remained active through most of the decade, working in tandem with his wife, but she was never again to receive a directorial credit.

Nell Shipman (1892-1970) spent some years with Vitagraph in the teens as both a writer and actress. She was quite a remarkable woman, making her first professional appearance as a soubrette in 1906 and going on to become a dramatic actress, scriptwriter, novelist, and film director. She was also a phenomenal self-publicist. The trade papers from the teens years contain innumerable items and photographs of Shipman, out of all proportion to her importance in the film industry.

Shipman's particular delight was the great outdoors, as typified by the Canadian wilderness—she was born in Victoria, British Columbia, Canada—where she set many of her productions. All of Nell Shipman's films possess a feel for nature and contain preachments for ecology in the days long before ecology meant anything. Her most famous film was *Back to God's Country*, directed by David Hartford, starring, produced and written by Nell Shipman, and based on a popular story by James Oliver Curwood. *Back to God's Country* was released on September 29, 1919; it was remade, not by Shipman, in 1927. Old-fashioned, quaint, and creaky by modern standards, it was obviously not too well oiled when first released. *Variety* (January 2, 1920) commented, "The picture is a meller of the real old-fashioned kind, and after reading the story and seeing the picture it seems that the James Oliver Curwood tales make better reading than they do screen material."

Shipman produced, co-directed (with Bert Van Tuyle), and starred in five further films: *Something New* (1920), *A Bear, a Boy and a Dog* (1921), *The Grub-Stake* (1922), *Little Dramas of the Big Places: Trail of the North Wind* (1923), and *Little Dramas of the Big Places: The Light on Lookout* (1923). Typical of these films is *Something New*, in which Shipman appears as herself—a writer outside at her typewriter—at the opening. She is a poor actress, coy and with bad teeth, and the production is amateurish in extreme. The titles are frightfully, aggressively modern, and thus seem old-fashioned. The bulk of the film—four out of its five reels—is concerned with Nell Shipman's rescue and escape from a band of Mexicans by car. The whole is obviously paid for by the car manufacturer, Maxwell (a brand much favored later by Jack Benny). At one point, Shipman is down on her knees, hugging the front of the car, with the name *Maxwell* clearly visible, and thanking the machine for all it has done. The story could have been told in two reels—and told a lot better.

It is ironic that while the films of so many early women directors have vanished, the productions of Nell Shipman survive and are widely screened. Because her autobiography has been published and because information on her is readily accessible, she has gained a prominence and importance out of all proportion to her worth. Yes, Nell Shipman was a prominent actress briefly in the teens, but her work as both a writer and director is negligible.[5]

Notes

1. Quoted in Monte M. Katterjohn, "Marguerite Bertsch of Vitagraph," *Photoplay*, vol. VI, no. 5, October 1914, p. 160.

2. Marguerite Bertsch, *How To Write for Moving Pictures: A Manual of Instruction and Information*, New York: George H. Doran Company, 1917.

3. Quoted in Stanley Olmsted, "Paula Blackton and Her Art," *Motion Picture Classic*, vol. IV, no. 1, March 1917, p. 54.

4. Quoted in Sue Roberts, "The Polly-Sidney Drew," *Motion Picture Magazine*, vol. XVII, no. 4, May 1919, p. 112.

5. Nell Shipman, *The Silent Screen & My Talking Heart*, Boise, ID: Boise State University, 1987. The Hemingway Western Studies Center at Boise State University has a number of Shipman films available for screening. It also distributes postcards of Shipman and scenes from her productions. The autobiography is unreadable.

Chapter Six

Margery Wilson

In recent times, Margery Wilson has been honored by film buffs for her performance as Brown Eyes, the young bride-to-be who is murdered in the French story from D. W. Griffith's *Intolerance*. Towards the end of her life, Miss Wilson liked to be remembered for the books that she had written and for her work as a counselor in the fields of self-improvement, personal esteem, and charm. One thing is certain. There are few likely to recall Margery Wilson, film director. But a film director she was, and a fairly good one by all accounts.

Margery Wilson was born Sarah Barker Strayer, in Gracey, Kentucky, on October 31, 1897. Her mother went into labor while "taking the waters" there, and Margery recalled, "I was born in such a hurry, the doctor barely had time to get to our house. And he just lived across the street. I was born in a hurry and I've been in a hurry ever since."[1] Wilson's mother was the head of the English and music departments at Sandy Valley Seminary in eastern Kentucky, and she encouraged her daughter to take part in amateur theatrical productions. "I was considered a 'child wonder' at elocutio —sometimes giving whole evenings of recitations," Wilson told me. "I was a 'diseuse' at the age of eleven and twelve—going out from Sandy Valley Seminary to give recitals for churches, clubs, etc. on a fifty-fifty basis. It came in most acceptably!"[2]

At the age of fourteen, Wilson obtained work as a leading lady with the John Lawrence Players in Cincinnati, Ohio. At the same time, rather than use her own name and bring disgrace on her family because of her profession, she became Margery Wilson in idolization of Woodrow Wilson's daughter, Margery. Late in 1914, Margery Wilson traveled to Los Angeles from Seattle, where she and her sister were appearing in musical comedy, to investigate the possibility of obtaining work for her sister in the film industry. On a visit to the Reliance-Mutual (later Fine Arts) Studio, she literally bumped into D. W. Griffith, and rather than sign her sister, he put Margery under contract.

It was Griffith's intention to have Margery Wilson portray St. Veronica, the young mother whose dead baby Christ brings back to life while en route to His crucifixion, in the Biblical sequence from *Intolerance*. The director also had another role planned for the actress, in the Babylonian story from *Intolerance*. As Wilson recalled in a 1919 interview, "I was to be a slave in the market-place who was a conscientious objector. But alas, Mr. Griffith cut out the whole series and the poor slave never got a chance to object."[3]

Eventually, the actress essayed the part of Brown Eyes in the French story, which dealt with the massacre of the Huguenots on St. Bartholomew's Eve. Playing opposite her was a young actor named Eugene Pallette, who was to gain great popularity as a character actor in Hollywood films of the 1930s and 1940s. The French sequence is overwhelmed by the modern and Babylonian stories, and, as Frederick James Smith pointed out in *The New York Dramatic Mirror* (September 16, 1916), "Margery Wilson has opportunity to reveal little more than prettiness as the Huguenot heroine." However, along with Miriam Cooper, Mae Marsh, and Constance Talmadge, Margery Wilson is one of the four heroines of *Intolerance* and certainly makes a major contribution to the film in comparison with Lilian Gish as "the hand that rocks the cradle."

Margery Wilson had much the same ethereal quality and delicate features as Lillian Gish, and as she grew older the likeness to Gish was even stronger. Back in October 1982, I was at Los Angeles International Airport with Margery Wilson and had to leave her temporarily to find a skycap. On my return, I found the actress surrounded by a group of travelers who were positive that she was Lillian Gish!

While under contract to D. W. Griffith, Margery Wilson appeared in two films, supervised but not directed by him, *Double Trouble* (1915, the second feature film to star Douglas Fairbanks) and *Bred in the Bone* (1915, with Dorothy Gish). Even during the filming of *Intolerance*, Griffith loaned the actress out to producer Thomas H. Ince, with her first Ince feature being the William S. Hart vehicle *The Primal Lure*, released on May 21, 1916. When Griffith realized he would have no further use for Wilson because of his planned visit to Europe to commence shooting *Hearts of the World*, in October 1916, he arranged for her to be put under contract to Ince's Triangle-Kay Bee Company.

She played opposite William S. Hart in four further films: *The Return of Draw Egan* (1916), *The Desert Man* (1917), *The Gun Fighter* (1917), and *Wolf Lowry* (1917). Margery Wilson was also featured in a score of Triangle releases, including *The Eye of the Night* (1916, with William H. Thompson), *The Sin Ye Do* (1916, with Frank Keenan), *The Last of the Ingrahams* (1917, with William Desmond), and *The Hand at the Window* (1918, with Joe Rock). Her most entertaining feature from this period is undoubtedly *The Clodhopper* (1917), in which she plays the stay-at-home girlfriend of Charles Ray. Late in 1919, Wilson left Triangle and played leading roles for Paramount in *Venus in the East* (1919), with Bryant Washburn, and for Pathé in *The House*

of Whispers (1920), with J. Warren Kerrigan. A few months
later, Margery Wilson became a director.

Her first venture as both director and star was *That
Something,* based on the 1915 book by W. W. Woodbridge,
dedicated to the Rotary Clubs of the World. As its director
explained, "'That Something' refers to that unnameable
thing that makes of a man a success or a failure." The film
was shot at the Robert Brunton Studios in Hollywood.
Miss Wilson remembered,

> When I went over to Mr. Brunton, who had handled
> all the sets, etc. for Thomas Ince—and that was where
> I met him—he had always been very friendly to
> me—he tried to discourage me from producing and
> directing. He said it would be bedlam, and that the
> actors and even the "grips" would just do as they
> pleased. But when he saw that he couldn't move me,
> he began to cooperate. He fixed up existing sets for
> my story and made it all possible, still shaking his
> head and saying I would lose my shirt, break my
> heart, and my health, etc.
>
> The first day on the set I called everybody together
> and told them the story and what I expected of each
> of them. I didn't know that Mr. Brunton was eaves-
> dropping. I told my group that if they had sugges-
> tions of any kind to give them to me *now* for after we
> started shooting I wanted not a single interruption.
> Everything went like clockwork—everybody was so
> interested we even forgot about lunch—but when we
> did go over to the commissary to eat, Mr. Brunton
> came over to the table and silent extended his hand,
> which I shook gravely.

Although shot in 1920, *That Something* was not released
until the spring of 1921, and then by the E. P. Hermann

Film Corporation, which had gained financial control of the production. "I lost control of that through interference," explained Margery. "I didn't lose control of the others; I had cut my teeth." *That Something* did, however, play at least one theatre in Los Angeles, the Victory, in May 1920.

The five-reel feature, starring Margery Wilson as Sarah Holmes and Charles Meredith as Edwin Drake, received favorable notices. *The Moving Picture World* (April 16, 1921) commented,

> New Thought, Will Power, "Pollyanaism" and a suggestion of *The Passing of the Third Floor Back* make up the ingredients of this production of the Hermann Film Corporation. Starting in a third-class boarding house and the purlieus of the underworld the story is concerned with the rise to wealth and position of the orphan slavey and the down-and-outer through "That Something" which is here shown as the power of "I will" in the human soul. The story is a consistent one. The chief fault in the direction lies in the sameness of action, which tends to monotony. Otherwise the production is a creditable one of its class.

On July 3, 1920, *The Moving Picture World* reported that Margery Wilson had begun work on a series of two-reel comedies, which she had also written, again at the Brunton Studios. The first of these comedies, *Two of a Kind*, was completed in the summer of 1920 and concerned two young boys who look alike. It might appear odd that Margery Wilson was so easily able to handle film direction, but as she explained,

> What most film people did not know was that I had had considerable experience directing on the stage. I

had my own stock company when I was sixteen years old! As I told in my autobiography, I put on long dresses at age fourteen—being tall—and got a job as leading lady with the John Lawrence Players in Cincinnati, Ohio. After two years, he went South, and the managers of the thearters we played in Covington and Newport, Kentucky, suggested that as I was the "backbone" of the company, that I just continue after Lawrence was gone! This I did—and made quite a bit of money. So I was accustomed to direction before I got to Hollywood. It seems incredible, but true—my whole life is incredible!

While with the John Lawrence Players, Margery Wilson made her first visit to Randolph, Vermont, staying with her friend, Katherine Holmes. She revisited the town on a number of later occasions, usually staying with Colonel Albert Brown Chandler and his wife, Marilla. It was Colonel Chandler who suggested to Wilson that she make two feature films on location in Vermont, *The Offenders* and *Insinuation*. Margery Wilson did not recall which production came first but believed it to be *The Offenders*. Nor did she recall the exact year in which the films were made. *The Offenders* was not released until 1924, whereas *Insinuation* was released in 1922. Since Margery Wilson's co-star in both films is Percy Helton, it seems highly probable that both were filmed at the same time. If *The Offenders* was filmed at a later date than *Insinuation,* it must have been prior to 1923, when Colonel Chandler died.

The Offenders, written by Katherine Holmes, concerned a heroine accused of a murder she did not commit and a "half-wit" whose testimony, after he is cured, saves the girl. In her autobiography, Margery Wilson recalled, "It consisted almost entirely of beautiful exterior shots and was better than it deserved to be, all things considered."[4]

Variety (November 12, 1924) was less than enthusiastic: "The story is weird. It has burglary, kidnapping, a couple of fights, murder, and a chase. Margery is the much abused heroine. Story horrible, direction terrible, acting awful."

Margery Wilson was the writer, director, and star of *Insinuation*. The film boasted a complicated plot of a young woman who takes money from her narrow-minded husband in order to cover up a robbery by her brother. When the husband divorces her, the woman is driven insane, but when she learns that her brother was innocent of any crime, she recovers and a reconciliation with her husband takes place. Margery Wilson had vivid memories of the production:

> I was the first person who ever made a film—not the Italians, not *The Bicycle Thief*, but Margery Wilson was the first person to make a film without a studio, without a single set. I was the first person in the wide world to do that, and the name of the picture was *Insinuation*. I wrote it, and directed it, and produced it, and acted in it, and sold it. I made over fifty thousand dollars, which I thought was a million at the time, now it would be nothing.
>
> I had done this before the Italians had ever thought of it, so this credit should stay in America, and not travel across, because I did it. I never thought about making history. I was just trying to save money, and I didn't see any reason to build a set that was already there. This picture was made in Vermont, and I had a whole carload of Kleig lights, spot lights and all that sort of thing, and took up an electrician. I arranged that we could tap the line anywhere. I moved these lights right into the actual rooms and homes.
>
> I had theater scenes there in Randolph, Vermont. I was the guest of Colonel Chandler, president of the

Postal Telegraph Cable Company. He told me to go
ahead and make the film, and he would pay for it. I
had the actors from New York. Oddly enough, I met
most of the actors I thought we needed face-to-face,
walking down Broadway. I had Percy Helton, who
played the crippled boy in *The Miracle Man*. He
played my brother in this film. I didn't pay anyone
by the week. I said, "What will you do this picture
for?" I said this to my cameraman, everyone on the
picture. I went to the electric company, and made a
deal with them for all the juice, electricity, that we
would need for the entire film. These three or four
men looked at me, and said would fifty dollars be too
much. I had to look down and hang on the table. So,
I paid them fifty dollars for all the electricity I needed
for the film. What they meant, of course, was that they
were so pleased I was going to give Vermont all this
advertising that they were practically giving it away.
I did everything on a flat basis. I didn't dare do it any
other way. I made it in the wintertime, and the scenes
were so incredibly beautiful, oh so beautiful. I
showed the film four times in Randolph, and people
came all four times They would have come every
night.

As with all of the films that Margery Wilson directed,
no print of *Insinuation* is known to exist, a tragic loss in that
it was her finest achievement. A fire in a New Jersey film
vault destroyed the negative, and the last remaining print
was stolen from a storage locker used by Wilson. *The
Moving Picture World* (September 2, 1922) wrote well of
Insinuation:

It is absolutely refreshing to review a picture like
Insinuation, whose real value and appeal lie, at its

outset, in its naturalness and which does not have to rely upon artificiality or luxurious props to aid in the telling of the story. In reality, *Insinuation* is a page taken bodily from the book of life itself, in fact several pages, and the story they tell is natural, wholesome, and absolutely faithful in detail and delineation. The plot of the picture-story is laid amid magnificent mountain scenery that is even more beautiful when covered with a mantle of snow....It is not too much to say, however, that in the last analysis *Insinuation* will be classified as among the top-notchers, and that the exhibitor who is fortunate enough to obtain it for his patrons not alone is going to be able to please those patrons, but is sure to add to his own reputation as a picker of the worth-while.

Margery Wilson embarked on a lengthy personal appearance tour with *Insinuation*, lasting three years, throughout the United States and Canada. She was particularly well received in Nova Scotia, where the *Halifax Evening Mail* wrote of her,

Margery Wilson is enshrined in the hearts of her Halifax admirers, not simply because she is a screen star, but just because she is plain Margery Wilson, gifted by nature with all the wonderful qualities which enable her to carry her audience spellbound with her through the narrative of love, sorrow, malice, and finally triumphant joy. *Insinuation* is a human story in which the star and each and every member of the supporting cast are distinctly human.

Marriage forced Margery Wilson's retirement from the screen: "I married a man who didn't want me to do anything." Required by her husband to stay at home, Wilson adapted her life and began a new career as a writer. She began by writing about the film industry, and as early as 1928, the Los Angeles-based Chimes Press published her monograph on Dolores Del Rio. In all, Margery Wilson authored an autobiography, *I Found My Way* (J. B. Lippincott, 1956) and an additional thirteen volumes on the subject that she generally described as "joyous living": *Charm* (Frederick A. Stokes, 1930), *The New Etiquette: The Modern Code of Social Behavior* (Frederick A. Stokes, 1937), *Your Personality — and God* (Frederick A. Stokes, 1938), *Make up Your Mind* (Frederick A. Stokes, 1940), *The Woman You Want to Be: The Complete Book of Charm* (J. B. Lippincott, 1942), *How to Live Beyond Your Means* (J. B. Lippincott, 1945), *How to Make the Most of Your Wife* (J. B. Lippincott, 1947), *Believe in Yourself* (J. B. Lippincott, 1949), *You're as Young as You Act: A Manual of Movement, Moods and Mannerisms* (J. B. Lippincott, 1951), *Double Your Energy and Live without Fatigue* (Prentice-Hall, 1961), and *Kinetic Psycho-Dynamics: How To Set the Amazing Powers of Your Mind into Motion* (Prentice-Hall, 1963).

Margery Wilson died in Arcadia, California, on January 21, 1986. She always displayed such a positive attitude towards life that she would ridicule any suggestion that she, as a woman, was not capable of handling any situation or activity while at the same time denying feminism and any loss of femininity in her behavior. She was obviously proud of the fact that her actions and her thoughts could not be categorized as those of a woman. In her autobiography, she relates a couple of incidents that prove her point, beginning after her direction of *That Something*:

When the picture was finished, I took it over and ran it for Mr. [Frank] Woods, who had given me my first chance in Hollywood and was now at Paramount. When the lights came up, he said, "It's excellent. Who directed it for you, Margery?" In surprise, I said, "Why, I did. Didn't you see the title—directed by Margery Wilson?" "Yes, I saw that," he said. "But Margery, no woman directed that picture. No woman has that much clarity of mind. That is a man's job."

Tears of rage welled into my eyes, I remembered the other times that sound thinking had been termed "a man's thinking."And there would be repetitions in the future. Years later, after a speech before the Rotary Club, I went down in the elevator with Ham Beal, the great publicity man, and he asked me, "Who wrote your speech, Margery?" I said, "Nobody, I spoke extemporaneously. I plotted it out a little." He patted my shoulder, "All right, dear, have it your way—but no woman on earth wrote that speech. Women don't think that way!"[5]

Notes

1. Quoted in Marjorie Ryerson, "Margery Wilson and The Colonel: A Music Hall's Bright Beginning," *White River Valley Herald,* September 2, 1982, p. B-1.

2. This and all other subsequent uncredited quotes are taken from an interview with Anthony Slide, July 12, 1972.

3. Quoted in Helen Morton, "Brains, Brown Eyes and Buttons," *Motion Picture Magazine,* vol. XVII, no. 2, March 1919, p. 31.

4. Margery Wilson, *I Found My Way,* Philadelphia: J. B. Lippincott, 1956, p. 196.

5. Ibid., pp. 184-185.

Chapter Seven

Mrs. Wallace Reid

The majority of women filmmakers were proud to be known by their own names. As married professionals, they generally used their maiden names. The one exception was Dorothy Davenport, who in a clear and very calculated manner decided to bill herself as Mrs. Wallace Reid and thus take advantage of the fame and scandal connected to her husband, one of the most popular male stars in the early years of the film industry, noted for his virility, easy charm, and good looks.

Born in Boston on March 13, 1895, Dorothy Davenport was the daughter of famous acting parents, Harry and Alice Davenport, and Dorothy made her stage debut in her mother's company, at the age of sixteen. She made her screen debut in 1910 with the American Biograph Company, later moving to Universal, where she was hailed by *The Universal Weekly* (September 28, 1912) as "one of the youngest, prettiest, classiest and most bewitching actresses appearing in motion pictures."

Wallace Reid and Dorothy Davenport were married in Los Angeles on October 12, 1913, while both were working for Universal. Reid was already a fairly popular leading man as a result of his earlier work at Vitagraph, but he became a star because of his performance in a small role, that of Jeff, the blacksmith, in D. W. Griffith's *The Birth of a Nation* (1915). Stripped to the waist in the part, Reid was able to show off his physique and his prowess in handling a brutal fight sequence. Jesse L. Lasky and Cecil B. DeMille saw the actor at the film's Los Angeles premiere and signed Reid to a long-term contract with Famous Players-Lasky. Wallace Reid became the company's biggest male star. Unfortunately, in 1919, while heading on location to film *The Valley of the Giants*, the actor was involved in a train wreck. Injured by falling debris, he was given morphine to ease the pain and became addicted to the drug. Eventually, the morphine led to his death, at the height of his fame, on January 18, 1923, at the age of thirty-one.

In 1922 Reid entered a sanitarium, and his wife called a press conference to announce his addiction. The response from the press and the public was remarkably sympathetic. There was shock that an actor who had typified the all-American hero on screen should be a drug addict, but there were no recriminations addressed to Reid. Public support was firmly behind the actor. Mrs. Reid told DeWitt Bodeen:

> I had nine wonderful years of the best with Wally, I wouldn't trade anything from them. Wally died very young—but he gave freely of the gifts of his youth. Most of all, he loved people, and the public responded in kind. He was much loved. He had so many talents—the gods were overly kind, but they also made him vulnerable, his own worst enemy, to compensate for their lavishness. He knew too much—and not enough.[1]

In reality, there is a strong possibility that the marriage between Reid and Dorothy Davenport was not a happy one. Off the record, Wallace Reid's leading lady at Famous Players-Lasky, Bebe Daniels, indicated that the couple's relationship was far from amicable, and that Reid was possibly bisexual or homosexual. Any or all of these may well have led to his welcoming morphine as a release from the problems of his domestic life. He made no effort to fight his addiction until it was too late, until the ravages of the drug were obvious in his appearance on screen.

There seems to be a cool and cynical calculation in the actions Mrs. Reid took as her husband lay dying. She used his illness to promote herself a career, and while it may have been a necessary step, in that she had two young children to raise, there is the distinct possibility that it was engineered to restore herself to the limelight from which she had been shaded by her husband's popularity.

Mrs. Reid established the Wallace Reid Foundation Sanitarium in the Santa Monica Mountains of Southern California, "for the cure of unfortunate drug addicts,"[2] and also accepted an offer from producer Thomas H. Ince to produce and star in an anti-narcotics film, *Human Wreckage*. It is generally stated that after Reid's death, Mrs. Reid and Adela Rogers St. Johns visited Washington, D.C., to attend a conference on narcotics. Upon her return to Los Angeles, Mrs. Reid decided to make *Human Wreckage*. In reality, *Human Wreckage*—which was released on June 17, 1923—may have been in the planning stages prior to the actor's passing.

Produced in cooperation with the Los Angeles Bureau of Drug Addiction, *Human Wreckage* was dedicated to Wallace Reid: "In humble tribute to the memory of A MAN who fought the leering curse of powdered death and, dying, was victorious." The script by C. Gardner Sullivan was based on an original story, "Dope," by Will Lambert, and the production was directed by Ince's top contract director of the period, John Griffith Wray (who that same year also directed the first screen version of Eugene O'Neill's *Anna Christie*). Even with competent if uninspired technicians such as Sullivan and Wray involved, it is obvious that Mrs. Reid had much to do with the making of the film. She recalled for me, "I did a great deal of work on the script; the supervision, trying to keep it as realistic as possible. I thought it came out well. I thought it accomplished its purpose. It was not just a contribution to the picture business, but a contribution to a cause."

Mrs. Wallace Reid was paid $500.00 a week while the film was in production and received a percentage of the net profit. She was also paid an additional $500.00 a week to make personal appearances with *Human Wreckage*. Such appearances apparently paid off at the box-office. At the Adams Theater, Detroit, the film grossed $14,000 a week with Mrs. Reid and $13,000 without her. At the Royal, Kansas City, with Mrs. Reid in attendance, *Human Wreckage* broke the house record, taking in $22,000 in one week. In New York, the distributor, Film Booking Offices of America, rented the Lyric Theater for four weeks at $4,000 a week. The first week, the film grossed $6,500, but after that ticket sales fell, and ultimately, taking into account publicity costs, the film closed to a net loss of $18,000.

The plotline of *Human Wreckage* (which is now a "lost" film) has an attorney (played by James Kirkwood) accidentally becoming addicted to morphine. Only when his wife (Dorothy Reid) shows signs of becoming an addict does the attorney gain the moral strength to shake off the habit. A strong supporting cast included Bessie Love and various Los Angeles civic leaders, including Dr. R. B. von Kleinsmid, president of the University of Southern California; Brigadier C. R. Boyd of the Salvation Army; and Los Angeles police chief Louis D. Oaks.

Despite its depressing and propagandistic theme, *Human Wreckage* was well received by the critics. *The Moving Picture World* (July 14, 1923) described it as "a picture that holds your attention and forcibly delivers its message." Of

Mrs. Reid's performance as the attorney's wife, Ethel MacFarland, *The World* continued, "Her presence on the screen establishes a deep note of realism and sincerity of purpose and her work in the role of the devoted wife keeps ever before you her own experiences." *Photoplay* (September 1923) described the film as "Not a cheery story for the whole family, and yet a picture that will probably do the old world a lot of good. The drug evil has never known so stiff a celluloid uppercut."

To criticize a Wallace Reid production was unthinkable. On the second anniversary of his death, James R. Quirk, editor of *Photoplay*, told of one lonely old lady who told him, "I am always happy when I see Wally's pictures. I never had children, but I keep thinking that he is my boy."[3] Similarly, *Human Wreckage* was above reproach. In the *Los Angeles Examiner*, Elinor Glyn wrote,

Human Wreckage filled me with deep emotion, I would like to cry aloud to every one who will see it in the coming weeks:

Look at it with the eyes of your souls. See in it an exposition of a fearful evil brought you through the anguish of a woman's heart. It is a sincere effort to awaken the American Nation—and all the other nations through which moving pictures circulate—to a menace which can sap the vitality of the human race.

Try to remember Wallace Reid whom you all loved, as he used to be—generous and gallant and young—and, oh, so beautiful!—and think of his hideously tragic end—hunted to the death by that BEAST.

To criticize technicalities in *Human Wreckage* would be like criticizing the prayers of a child. Let it go forth unhampered to spread its message—and who knows—far away in shadowland, that soul, whose agonized passage inspired its production, may find peace.

There is considerable doubt as to whether the crew on *Human Wreckage* took the production or its message too seriously. A still photograph exists showing the all-male company, including director and cinematographer, enjoying simulated drug use with a variety of paraphernalia, including an opium pipe and syringe.

Mrs. Reid produced one further feature for Ince, *Broken Laws*, based on an original story by Adela Rogers St. Johns, which went into production on August 18, 1924, and was released on November 9 of the same year. Her director on this film, in which Mrs. Reid also starred, was Roy William Neill. *Broken Laws* was dedicated to the mothers of America, as a reminder that the foundation of all law and order is the home. It was an attack on neglectful parents, who indulged the whims of their children instead of giving them a good spanking. "It is a picture that children as well as parents should see and one that will impress and please," commented *The Moving Picture World* (January 31, 1925), "for it has the rare combination of being vastly entertaining, putting over a forceful lesson and making you think, and you will continue to think of it long after you have seen the picture."

Variety (February 4, 1925) praised the production:

Pictures expounding a definite "moral" often defeat their own aims by overstepping the limits of propriety in illustrating too freely the very evils they are trying to remedy. *Broken Laws* doesn't and it must be rated as a straight-from-the-shoulder, absorbing film, in which Mrs. Wallace Reid gives a most sincere performance. ...

Broken Laws should obtain its greatest play in the smaller cities and towns, where the attention of women's clubs and church societies can be focused upon it. While it goes thoroughly into the alleged vices of the present-day generation, it does not make the mistake of laying the sex and booze angles on too heavily, thus avoiding any loopholes for criticism on the grounds of frankness.

In 1925, Mrs. Wallace Reid formed her own production company, and began work on *The Red Kimono*, adapted by Dorothy Arzner from an original story by Adela Rogers St. Johns. The direction was in the hands of Walter Lang—his first assignment—but Mrs. Reid sat next to him on the set throughout the production and approved each take. Playing the leading role was ingenue Priscilla Bonner, who became a lifelong friend of Mrs. Reid. She recalled the film as "a crusade. She thought it was good to go from dope to 'let those without sin cast the first stone.'"[4]

The film opens with Mrs. Reid in the "morgue" of a newspaper office, where she opens a 1917 newspaper on the story of Gabrielle Darley (Priscilla Bonner). The latter is first seen in the "crib" district of New Orleans, where she learns that her boyfriend has left for Los Angeles to marry another woman. She follows, and finding him in a jewelry store buying a wedding ring, she shoots him. At the trial, the girl tells the sorry story of a life in which she was lured into prostitution. A sympathetic judge acquits the girl, who, in an unintentionally amusing scene, walks past a Red Cross poster, announcing, "At the service of all mankind." Gabrielle is taken in by a wealthy socialite, but once she tires of the girl as a novelty, Gabrielle is asked to leave. About to return to her old life in the "crib," Gabrielle decides instead to do her part for the war effort by working in a hospital. As she is cleaning the floor, the socialite's chauffeur, who had fallen in love with her, enters. He is about to go overseas on military service and wants to marry her, but Gabrielle tells him that he must wait until she is completely regenerated. The film concludes with a suitable biblical quotation from Mrs. Reid.

Critical response was very negative. *Variety* (February 3, 1926) recalled that it was films such as *The Red Kimono* that had put back the German film industry ten years and noted, "Mrs. Reid or someone else may believe she is doing something for the fallen woman in turning out a picture of this sort, but the chances are that she will do tremendous harm to the picture industry as a whole and to herself." *Photoplay* (March 1926) described *The Red Kimono* as "Something terrible. It started out with a good story by Adela Rogers St. Johns and was directed by Mrs. Wallace Reid. But somewhere the great qualities of those ladies' talents got completely lost." In the *New York Times* (February 3, 1926), Mordaunt Hall wrote, "There have been a number of wretched pictures on Broadway during the last year, but none seem to have quite reached the low level of *The Red Kimono*." The only positive comment concerned Priscilla Bonner and that came from Arthur James in *Variety* (December 26, 1925):

Put *The Red Kimono* right up in the front row as a box-office production and weave a wreath of fame for Priscilla Bonner who, for consistent acting, appealing personality and a developed talent takes her place among the foremost actresses of the screen. Priscilla Bonner has a Gish quality with a greater vitality and in a role requiring the utmost delicacy to conserve its sympathy she demonstrates unusual power. Cast in the right roles and well directed, this young woman has no handicap to place her at the top rung of the ladder.

The contemporary criticism seems strangely misplaced. Viewed today, *The Red Kimono* is a strong production, lacking the melodramatics that one might expect from such a story. Mrs. Reid deserves considerable praise for her refusal to condemn Gabrielle Darley and her lifestyle. Not once is the suggestion made that Darley might have chosen anything other than prostitution, and the chauffeur-hero does not condemn her when she considers returning to that life. Aside from Louis Malle's *Pretty Baby* (1978), *The Red Kimono* is perhaps the only feature film to document the Storyville district of New Orleans, named after Mayor Story, who attempted to confine all crime—drugs, gambling, prostitution, and the like—to one area of the city. The expensive prostitutes were listed in the "Blue Book," while the poorer ones, such as Gabrielle Darley, maintained one-room shacks, called cribs. (The slang term, *to crib*, meaning "to cheat," derives from the cribs of New Orleans, where men might crib or cheat on their wives.)

One of the "selling points" for *The Red Kimono* was that it was based on a true story. Gabrielle Darley really existed. Unfortunately, she was very much alive. She had been tried for murder and acquitted, and, in 1919, she married Bernard Melvin of St. Louis. When she saw *The Red Kimono*, Darley, who had become a respected member of the community, was outraged. She sued for $50,000, claiming that the showing of the film to her friends had made them aware for the first time of her unsavory earlier life and caused them to scorn and abandon her. It was one of the first times that a lawsuit had been filed in the matter of one's right to privacy, unknown in common law. The case was eventually settled in Darley's favor in 1931, when the District Court of Appeal, Fourth District, California, questioned a defendant's right to privacy but did conclude that *The Red Kimono* violated Darley's right "to pursue and obtain happiness," as guaranteed by the Constitution of California.[5]

Had Mrs. Reid taken the simple expediency of changing the name of her heroine, there would have been no lawsuit, but as it was, Mrs. Reid started the 1930s penniless, losing even the family home in West Hollywood.

Unaware of a potential lawsuit, Mrs. Reid began production of a second feature, *The Earth Woman*, again directed by Walter Lang, and starring Priscilla Bonner, and released by Associated Exhibitors on April 4, 1926. Bonner recalls that the film was "thrown together" very quickly in an effort to reap the rewards from the popular success of *The Red Kimono*. A lurid melodrama, involving murder, lynching, alcoholism, and horsewhipping, *The Earth Woman* was dedicated to "the toilers of the soil, the homesteaders who struggled to conquer the wilderness."

The Earth Woman was neither a popular nor a critical success. Noting it was set in Tennessee, "where moonshine is moonshine while men loaf and women work," *Variety* (June 23, 1926) praised Mary Alden in the role of the mother and recommended the film for "the daily change grind houses where the audiences are not too particular." *The Moving Picture World* (May 29, 1926) wrote, "This rather drab and cheerless story has little of comedy relief, the appeal is concentrated on the forceful drama of elemental persons and passions and the production is marked by well-drawn and interesting characterizations admirably handled by an excellent cast."

For the next two years, Mrs. Reid returned to acting with leading roles in two minor productions from an equally minor producer, Gotham. In *The Satan Woman*, released on August 1, 1927, she was directed by her old friend Walter Lang. *Hellship Bronson*, released in May 1928, had Mrs. Reid opposite Noah Beery, under the direction of Joseph Henabery.

Mrs. Wallace Reid Productions was resurrected in 1929 for *Linda*, the first film on which Mrs. Reid was credited as director. Released on April 1, 1929, *Linda* featured Warner Baxter, Helen Foster, and Noah Beery in a tale of a young girl forced to marry against her will. Basically a silent film with a synchronized music score, sound effects, and a theme song, *Linda* opened at the Lincoln Square Theater, New York, on April 1, 1929. It was described by *Variety* (April 3, 1929) as a "nicely put together backwoods story that should get money...despite the fact that the flicker has all the evidences of being a quickie." Following production of *Linda* and after some promotional work on a 1930 Sono-Art production, *The Dude Wrangler*, Mrs. Reid announced her retirement.

However, a woman such as Mrs. Wallace Reid could not be expected to retire permanently, for, as one writer put it, "retiring is not so easy for a small dynamo with an idea per minute."[6] It was also not too easy for anyone at the wrong end of a major lawsuit. In 1933, Mrs. Reid returned to the film industry, not to work for any of the major studios, but to direct, produce, and write for a number of poverty-row companies.

Her first assignment was as co-director, with Melville Shyer, on a 1933 Willis Kent production titled *Sucker Money*. Of this feature, starring Mischa Auer, Phillis Barrington, and Ralph Lewis, *The Film Daily* (March 1, 1933) wrote, "There's plenty of action, suspense, thrills and good old-fashioned melodrama in this story showing up the mystic seance fakery, and the subject is one that can be exploited to good advantage."

In 1934, Mrs. Reid directed two features—*The Road to Ruin* for True Life Photoplays and *The Woman Condemned* for Marcy Pictures. "This is a murder mystery drama which after maintaining interest fairly well ends on a climax that leaves the mystery somewhat unexplained," wrote *The Film Daily* (April 20, 1934) of *The Woman Condemned*, starring Claudia Dell, Lola Lane, Jason Robards, and Mischa Auer. *The Road to Ruin*, co-directed again with Melville Shyer, was the classic tale of a young girl's moral downfall. *The Film Daily* (February 21, 1934) commented,

> The old story of young girls following the primrose path is honestly and frankly handled, without any suggestive scenes. It is a frank presentation of the pitfalls of youth, and it whitewashes none of the characters. The results of their folly, ignorance and carelessness are pointed graphically for the moral.

Mrs. Wallace Reid took time out in 1934 to talk about the role of women in the film industry: "The first thing a woman producer must do is take the sex out of executive work. Either men are too polite and spare her the truth, or they go to the other extreme and have no consideration for legitimate foibles."

When asked as to what a woman executive could do to defeat antagonism towards her, Mrs. Reid replied,

> She can use the fact that she *is* a woman to motivate things. That is, to take deliberate advantage of the theory that women must have a certain consideration not accorded men. Then, it is up to her to follow through with what she has to give. She simply uses the feminine viewpoint for her *approach*, but she must go from there to masculine attack and execution.
>
> Before this, my experience had been with my own money. What I said had to go. Now I must work that much harder to convince that my slant is sound. I believe it takes a woman to believe in a woman's motives, and every story intended for the screen should have a woman working on it at some stage, to

convince the audience of women. Later, also, everything a man does on the screen is done to please a
woman or women. Actors say to me, "You tell me
what you think in this scene." Where, if they were
asking a man, they would be more apt to say, "Tell
me what to do." A man and a woman, working
together on the story, can hit a better emotional angle.
For example, a man only knows that he gets fed up
with a woman, but he doesn't know *why*. A woman,
writing the story, has feminine vision into all the little
irritations that cause it.[7]

In 1934, Mrs. Reid began a long association with Monogram. She produced *Redhead*, directed by Melville Brown,
and the following year, she produced her last film, *Honeymoon Limited*, directed by Arthur Lubin. *Honeymoon Limited* was the beginning of a long partnership with Lubin,
with Mrs. Reid working in a production and writing capacity on many of the director's films through the 1950s;
from 1950-1956, she helped write the *Francis the Talking
Mule* series that Lubin produced for Universal. While she
was no longer a producer or a director, there were many
other opportunities for this remarkably resilient woman
in the 1930s. She wrote the scripts for *Women Must Dress*
(1935), *Prison Break* (1938), *Drums of the Desert* (1940),
Haunted House (1940), *The Old Swimmin' Hole* (1940), *On the
Spot* (1940), and *Tomboy* (1940). She was story supervisor
on the first Republic Pictures feature, *Forbidden Heaven*, in
1935, and also *Two Sinners* (1935), directed by Lubin. She
supervised production of *The House of a Thousand Candles*
for Republic in 1936, and was associate producer of Monogram's *A Bride for Henry* in 1937. In 1938, Mrs. Reid scripted
and served as associate producer on Monogram's *Rose of
the Rio Grande*, and the previous year she was both associ-

ate producer and second unit director on location in Samoa for the same company's *Paradise Isle*.

As late as the 1970s, she described herself only as "semi-retired." She was still willing to work, but as she told me, when I was writing the original edition of *Early Women Directors*, "for the last couple of years, I am just being lazy. They were great fun days. I loved the business. It wasn't arduous; it was just fun."

Mrs. Reid's son, Wallace Reid, Jr., became an actor in the 1930s, starring in the 1932 Willis Kent Production, *The Racing Strain*, for which his mother provided the story. He was later a successful architect.

Notes

1. DeWitt Bodeen, "Wallace Reid," *Films in Review*, vol. XVII, no. 4, April 1966, p. 220.

2. "A Remarkable Monument to Wally Reid's Memory," *Photoplay*, vol. XXVI, no. 4, September 1924, p. 74.

3. James R. Quirk, "Speaking of Pictures," *Photoplay*, vol. XXVII, no. 4, March 1925, p. 27.

4. Interview with Anthony Slide, July 13, 1974.

5. Melvin V. Reid et al., Civ. 346, District Court of Appeal, Fourth District, California, February 28, 1931.

6. Ruth Rankin, "Mrs. Reid Comes Back," *Shadowplay*, December 1934.

7. Ibid.

Chapter Eight

Frances Marion

Frances Marion's contribution to the cinema has been considerable; she was undoubtedly one of the most important screenwriters of all time. She is a perfect example of just how important women once were in the film industry. A list of the films which she scripted reads like a table of the screen's greatest productions: *Stella Maris* (1917), *Rebecca of Sunnybrook Farm* (1917), *Pollyanna* (1920), *Humoresque* (1920), *Secrets* (1924), *Graustark* (1925), *Stella Dallas* (1925), *The Scarlet Letter* (1926), *The Wind* (1928), *Anna Christie* (1930), *The Big House* (1930), *Min and Bill* (1930), *Dinner at Eight* (1933), *Camille* (1937) — the list is endless. Apart from D. W. Griffith, she worked for practically every major silent director; Maurice Tourneur, Frank Borzage, Victor Seastrom, Marshall Neilan, Allan Dwan, James Cruze, John Ford, etc.

Adela Rogers St. Johns has written of Frances Marion, "As a writer, she is unquestioned head of her profession, male or female, and the proof is in the pictures to which her name is signed, and in the box office returns on those pictures."[1]

But it is as a director that this book is concerned with Frances Marion, and as a director she was not one of the greatest, competent as she might have been. She directed only three features —*The Love Light, Just around the Corner,* and *The Song of Love*—a number that may indicate that she had no real love for directing. Unfortunately, Frances Marion's autobiography, *Off with Their Heads!* offers no indication of Miss Marion's thoughts on directing. As Gloria Swanson notes in her foreword to the book, "She tells us little enough about herself."[2]

Born, Frances Marion Owens, in San Francisco, on November 18, 1890, Frances Marion entered the film industry through the encouragement of Lois Weber. Weber engaged Marion as an actress and script girl in 1914 and generally looked upon her as a protégé.

Frances Marion directed her first film, *Just around the Corner*, at the request of William Randolph Hearst, for his Cosmopolitan Company in 1920. She had already successfully scripted one film for Hearst, based on a Fannie Hurst novel, *Humoresque*, and no one opposed her choice of a second Hurst story for her directorial debut.

Featuring Margaret Seddon and Lewis Sargent, hardly two of the silent screen's most prominent players, *Just around the Corner* was not released, by Paramount, until December 11, 1921. It received reasonably favorable reviews. *The Moving Picture World* (January 24, 1922) commented

> *Just around the Corner* is human drama, a warm, sympathetic study of the home life of an East Side family. Adapted by Frances Marion from Fannie Hurst's story about New York, and also directed by Miss Marion, its slight plot has been stretched into a Cosmopolitan Production of feature length, with few obvious evidences of "padding." The picture has hardly a trace of melodrama, though several of the situations give promise of it, depending for its appeal upon characterization and heart interest rather than action. It succeeds in reaching the heart through its

excellent acting, even continuity and faithful portrayal of typical incidents in the lives of poor people.

For her next directorial-cum-writing effort, *The Love
Light*, Frances Marion was reunited with an old friend,
Mary Pickford. Frances Marion had first worked with
Pickford as an actress in *A Girl of Yesterday*, in 1915. The
following year, she had written her first original scenario,
The Foundling, and its star was Mary Pickford. Marion
wrote some of Pickford's greatest successes, and as Adela
Rogers St. Johns commented, "It isn't the slightest exag-
geration to say that without Frances Marion there would
have been no Mary Pickford."[3]

The Love Light was produced by Mary Pickford, and
released by United Artists on January 9, 1921. Playing
opposite Pickford was Frances Marion's second husband,
clergyman-turned actor Fred Thomson, who had made his
screen debut in *Just around the Corner* and who was to
become a popular cowboy star. Frances Marion recalled
for DeWitt Bodeen that *The Love Light* "was a challenge in
more ways than one, Mary had never been directed by a
woman, and my story offered her a highly dramatic role."[4]

Frances Marion turned away from the "sweetness and
light" characters that Pickford had earlier played and
wrote a story in which the actress was required to play
high melodrama. Here she is an Italian named Angela,
responsible for the lighthouse in a small Italian fishing
village, while her brothers are away at the front during the
First World War. When a foreign sailor is washed ashore,
she takes care of him, and the couple marry, with Angela's
not knowing that he is a German spy, responsible for the
death of one of her brothers. A baby is born and given
away, the German dies, and Angela's sweetheart returns,
blinded by the war.

The direction is faultless, as good as the work of the male directors who had earlier worked with Pickford, but the storyline was too much for contemporary critics and audiences. They wanted the Pickford of old. One of the few positive reviews came from *The Moving Picture World* (January 22, 1921), in which Louis Reeves Harrison wrote,

> *The Love Light* is a play of adventure full of outward movement, yet motivated by love and tempered by humor, a romance verging on romantic tragedy. The story will excite unusual attention from the fact that Mary Pickford has made a departure in the interest of variety, a departure from ingenue roles of comedy, a change which many will welcome....Her support is one of great excellence, especially in the Italian types, and the atmosphere provided by Director Frances Marion leaves nothing to be desired in the way of artistic backgrounds.

Pickford went back to playing the parts with which she was most associated, and Marion would soon return to writing the same, rather tired old stories with which, in hindsight, her name is generally linked. It is very obvious that there are elements of Madame Butterfly in *The Love Light*, and this would seem to be a favorite theme of Marion's for she used it in her 1922 script for the first Technicolor feature, *The Toll of the Sea*.

Frances Marion directed only one further film, *The Song of Love*, in collaboration with Chester Franklin (director of *The Toll of the Sea*). Released on December 21, 1923, the production featured Norma Talmadge and Joseph Shildkraut and involved an Arab sheik and his plans to drive the French out of North Africa. Produced by Norma Talmadge's own company, which she co-owned with Joseph M. Schenck, *The Song of Love* was not one of the star's best films. As *The Moving Picture World* (January 19, 1924) pointed out, "while it provides entertainment above the average, it...is somewhat of a disappointment because of what we have learned to expect in Miss Talmadge's productions."

It is interesting to note the power that women had in the film industry at this time. Frances Marion's last two films both featured women stars with their own producing companies, who had carte blanche as to story, director, and supporting players.

Frances Marion continued as a screenwriter until as late as 1940, when she scripted James Whale's *Green Hell* at Universal. Her final screen credit was in 1953 on M-G-M's *The Clown*, to which she contributed the original story. She had seen many changes in the film industry, including the decline of female power. She told DeWitt Bodeen,

> I don't think Hollywood will ever again be as glam-
> orous, or as funny, or as tragic, as it was during the
> teens, the twenties and the thirties. But that's what
> everybody says about the past as he grows older and
> looks back on the days of his youth, when everything
> was new and exciting and beautiful. Was it really that
> way? Frankly, too often, all I can remember are the
> heartbreak and the hard work.[5]

Aside from her work as a screenwriter and whilom film director, Frances Marion authored some five novels— *Minnie Flynn* (Boni and Liveright, 1925), *Valley People* (Reynal & Hitchcock, 1935), *Molly, Bless Her* (Harper & Bros., 1937), *Westward the Dream* (Doubleday, 1948), and *Powder Keg* (Little, Brown, 1953)—together with a textbook on screenwriting, *How to Write and Sell Film Stories* (Covici, Friede, 1937), and an autobiography, *Off with Their Heads!: A Serio-Comic Tale of Hollywood* (Macmillan, 1972).

On May 12, 1973, Frances Marion died in Los Angeles. In its obituary, the *New York Times* described her as the dean of Hollywood screenwriters. In 1934, Marion's close friend, Adela Rogers St. Johns wrote of her, "As a woman, she is a philanthropist, a patroness of young artists, and herself the most brilliant, versatile and accomplished person in Hollywood."[6] Frances Marion could ask no better epitaph.

Notes

1. Adela Rogers St. Johns, "The One Genius in Pictures—Frances Marion," *Silver Screen*, vol. IV, no. 3, January 1934, p. 22.

2. Frances Marion, *Off with Their Heads!: A Serio-Comic Tale of Hollywood*, New York: Macmillan, 1972, pp. ix-x.

3. Adela Rogers St. Johns, "The One Genius in Pictures—Frances Marion," *Silver Screen*, vol. IV, no. 3, January 1934, p. 53.

4. DeWitt Bodeen, "Frances Marion," *Films in Review*, vol. XX, no. 2, February 1969, p. 85.

5. Ibid., vol. XX, no 3, March 1969, p. 143.

6. Adela Rogers St. Johns, "The One Genius in Pictures—Frances Marion," *Silver Screen*, vol. IV, no. 3, January 1934, p. 22.

Chapter Nine

Dorothy Arzner

There is no argument that Dorothy Arzner was a pioneer film director. The reason is not because she was the first female director or because she was the best, but rather because she was the only American woman director to make a successful transition from the silent era to sound, and she became a symbol for what women could accomplish in the new medium. The four silent and thirteen sound features that Arzner directed between 1927 and 1943 were creative examples for the women who followed. It might well be argued that had it not been for Dorothy Arzner, there would have been no incentive for later female directors in the film industry, such as Ida Lupino, Elaine May, or Joan Micklin Silver.

Dorothy Arzner is also unique in that unlike the silent women directors who proceeded her, she was a staunch feminist. Her films, particularly *Christopher Strong* (1933), show women in dominant roles. Her stars, including Clara Bow, Ruth Chatterton, Katharine Hepburn, Rosalind Russell, and Joan Crawford, were strong women. Indeed, one critic complained, in reviewing *Nana* (1934), that Dorothy Arzner was the Mae West of film direction, "that is, she's an exaggerated feminist, being gentle with the women and always giving men the worst of it."[1]

When Dorothy Arzner first decided to give up a successful career as a film editor to become a director, her screenwriter friend Beulah Marie Dix advised her that no woman would have the stamina to direct.[2] Paramount obviously felt much the same way in that the company gave Arzner, as her first directorial assignment, *Fashions for Women*, a film more concerned with the glamorization of the female sex than with putting over a worthwhile story.

However, Dorothy Arzner persevered. She directed one of Paramount's first talkies, *The Wild Party*, and never produced a film that was not, at the least, on a par, both commercially and artistically, with those of her male colleagues. As if to emphasize her lesbianism, to flaunt her sexual preference in front of the studio bosses, she wore cold, masculine attire on the set. It was as if she was determined to make a stand not only for feminism but also for lesbianism. There was no compromise. Unlike male directors such as George Cukor and Edmund Goulding, who were careful to mask their homosexuality, Dorothy Arzner was proud *and* courageous in an age when such attitudes were unacceptable, particularly with conservative studio executives. Even in the 1990s, there are few openly gay and lesbian filmmakers in Hollywood. It is a taboo that cannot and could not be broken—except by one brave woman some seven decades ago.

Why Dorothy Arzner retired from the screen will never really be known. Arzner always maintained that "pictures left me" and that she had had enough. Yet her penultimate film, *Dance, Girl, Dance*, made in 1940, is one of her best and shows that she had in no way lost her creative ability. Of course, Arzner continued to work, with Second World War documentaries, television commercials, and a teaching career at UCLA, where one of her pupils was Frances Ford Coppola.

She received a 1975 Directors Guild of America tribute, but, when all is said and done, by her death in 1979

Dorothy Arzner had been relatively forgotten. Since then, more and more women filmmakers have come to acknowledge their debut to Arzner. On January 24, 1986, she received a long-overdue "star" on the Hollywood Walk of Fame, and present at the ceremony were three women who recognized their indebtedness: Fay Kanin, screenwriter and former president of the Academy of Motion Picture Arts and Sciences; actress and filmmaker Lee Grant; and then-Paramount Pictures executive Dawn Steel.

Dorothy Arzner claimed to have been born in San Francisco on January 3, 1900, the daughter of an American father and a Scottish mother. Her birth record was lost in the San Francisco earthquake, and Arzner adopted 1900 as her birthdate, although the year was probably more likely to have been 1897. After the earthquake, the family moved down to Los Angeles, where Louis Arzner ran the Hoffman Cafe, famous for its German cooking and a favorite meeting place for members of the film community, including Charles Chaplin, William S. Hart, and Erich von Stroheim. "All of the early movie and stage actors came to my Dad's restaurant for dinner," Arzner told Gerald Peary and Karyn Kay. "I had no personal interest in actors because they were too familiar to me."[3]

It has been suggested that Arzner's close proximity to actors and actresses led to a fascination with the film industry, but this is hardly true in that after graduation from the prestigious Westlake girls school, she spent two years at the University of Southern California, studying to become a doctor. After deciding a life in medicine was not for her, Arzner joined a volunteer ambulance brigade in the vain hope that she might be sent to Europe. Instead, she met William C. de Mille, the sensitive and artistic director-brother of Cecil B. DeMille. He dissuaded Arzner from seeking a major position in the film industry, and she agreed to begin her career typing scripts at fifteen dollars a week. As Arzner later told Adela Rogers St. Johns,

> Sometimes, I think that pride is the greatest obstacle to success. A silly false pride, that keeps people from being willing to learn, from starting at the bottom no matter how far down it may be, and learning every step of the way up. When I went to work in a studio, I took my pride and made a nice little ball of it and threw it right out the window.[4]

Arzner must have taken time out from her typing duties at Famous Players-Lasky to work on the set of *Stronger Than Death*, starring Nazimova, directed by Herbert Blaché, and released in January 1920. She worked as script girl on the production and must have been attracted to the Nazimova feature because of its star's sexual preference, well-known within the industry. It has been claimed that Arzner was Nazimova's lover at the time, but this is an unsubstantiated statement, and Arzner does not appear to have been invited to stay around and work on Nazimova's independent productions, *A Doll's House* and *Salome*.

Stronger Than Death was shot at the Metro Studios in Hollywood, but in 1920, Arzner was back at Famous Players-Lasky, where Nan Heron encouraged her to become a cutter or a film editor. "She was cutting a Donald Crisp picture, *Too Much Johnson*," Arzner recalled.

> I watched her work on one reel and she let me do the second, while she watched and guided every cut. On Sunday I went into the studio and assembled the next reel. On Monday I told her about it and she looked at it and approved. I finished the picture under her guidance .[5]

Arzner was assigned to the Famous Players-Lasky subsidiary, Realart, and she claimed to have cut and edited fifty-two features for the company. As was fairly common practice at the time, she also worked as both a script girl and cutter on many of the films. "I learned more about pictures in the cutting room than anywhere else," Arzner told Adela Rogers St. Johns.[6]

Early in 1922, Arzner was asked to edit Fred Niblo's *Blood and Sand*, featuring Rudolph Valentino, and she also claims to have filmed some of the bullfight sequences. Director James Cruze, who had known Arzner back in the Hoffman Cafe days, was so impressed by her work on *Blood and Sand* that he invited her to edit his next production, *The Covered Wagon* (1923). Arzner also edited and served as script girl, on three further Cruze features, *Ruggles of Red Gap* (1923), *Merton of the Movies* (1924) and *Old Ironsides* (1926).

While working as an editor at Paramount, Dorothy Arzner had been writing scripts for a number of minor films elsewhere, including two for Harry Garson Productions, *The Breed of the North* (1924) and *The No-Gun Man* (1924), and *The Red Kimono* (1925) for Mrs. Wallace Reid Productions. She claimed to have written several for Harry Cohn's Columbia Pictures, although she receives credit on only one, *When Husbands Flirt* (1925). She informed Columbia that she wanted to direct her next script, and the studio agreed. Late on the day she was scheduled to say farewell to Paramount she passed producer Walter Wanger in the hallway. When she told him of her plans, he immediately discussed the matter with executive B. P. Schulberg, and the two men offered Arzner the opportunity to direct a Paramount feature with the working title of *The Best Dressed Woman in Paris*. The film, eventually released as *Fashions for Women*, was to be the first starring vehicle for Esther Ralston, who had been under contract to Paramount since 1924, when she played Mrs. Darling in *Peter Pan*.

Ralston played the dual role of Celeste de Givray and Lola Davry in this society drama of a cigarette girl who poses as a fashion model and is declared the best-dressed woman in Paris. The film was a remarkable commercial success, in large thanks to its leading lady, who was known to have box-office potential and enjoyed a lengthy career, lasting well into the sound era. Arzner's direction was not received with great enthusiasm. *The Moving Picture World* (April 9, 1927) commented,

> The production is the first offering of Dorothy Arzner, Paramount's new woman director. She seems to have been overeager to direct, and some of the scenes show this in their lack of spontaneity. The action is directed, rather than natural, but as a whole the novice has done well. She has produced a colorful background and introduced bales of charming frocks. Between dress and undress the play should please both sexes.

In a long review in *The Film Spectator* (May 28, 1927), Welford Beaton determined that Arzner had not been given a chance:

> When it decided to let her try her hand at directing Paramount might have given Dorothy Arzner a story with something in it. *Fashions for Women* is just about as scanty as the prevailing fashions for women. To that extent it is consistent. The manner in which most of the scenes are presented also is consistent with the theme. The characters, like the gowns, are cut off at the knees. I refuse to believe that there was not more merit in the direction than there was in the editing.

Bernie Fineman is credited with the supervision and Louis Lighton with the editing. Between them, if we are to judge them by this one picture, they seem to posses but slight knowledge of picture essentials. They had the sort of story that needed all the help it could get from its production, but they resorted to a multitude of close-ups which eliminate the production and leave the story to stand on its own weak legs. Also they deprive us of a full opportunity to judge Miss Arzner as a director, for anyone can direct close-ups. Most of those in this picture are meaningless. It is ridiculous to show characters walking around without any legs. To Miss Arzner's credit stands the ability she displays in handling ensemble shots. Her cafe sequences are life-like, and the fashion show looks like what I imagine a fashion show would look like. I never saw one, but I presume the people who attend them act like human beings instead of like those fascinating wax persons who adorn the windows of the shops down town, which the extras in most of such scenes so closely resemble in action, if they do no quite approach them in pulchritude....It could have been an amusing little affair with considerable pictorial value, but it lacks all the cleverness in treatment that such a story must have to make it convincing. And it looks to me as if its faults were things that the director was powerless to prevent.

The reviews of *Fashion for Women* notwithstanding, Dorothy Arzner was given a long-term contract by Paramount, and she remained with the studio through 1932, at which time it was reorganized and most of the contract players and directors were let go. Esther Ralston was again assigned as the star of Arzner's second feature, *Ten Modern Commandments* (also released in 1927), playing Kitten

O'Day, the maid in a theatrical boarding house. Yet again, the film was commercially successful. "The story is a bit thin as to plot," commented *The Moving Picture World* (July 27, 1927), "yet it is well laid out to get and hold attention, and is more true to the life than many backstage yarns."

Ten Modern Commandments marked the end of Arzner's working relationship with Esther Ralston. The actress was disturbed by some of the scenes that her director demanded she play, and even more so, by the obvious sexual advances made by Arzner. While Arzner may simply have been having good-natured fun in asking Esther Ralston to sit on her lap—she did the same thing to Clara Bow later—there is no question that by today's standards, such behavior would be labeled sexual harassment. Esther Ralston recalled,

I soon discovered that Dorothy Arzner was way ahead of her times. Looking back now, I feel she would have made some sensational "restricted" movies today, had she lived. But in those days of the Hays censorship, and being conscious of my public image as "Mrs. Darling," I began to resent some of the sexy scenes Arzner was asking me to do. The photographing of my backside and the display of my legs just wasn't me! One day, in rebellion, Arzner and I went to the front office to talk to our producer, Ben Schulberg. We each had our say and, thank goodness, Mr. Schulberg decided that I did not have to do any more suggestive scenes. Arzner never forgave me.

In May [of 1927], I started *Ten Modern Commandments*, with Neil Hamilton as leading man and again with Dorothy Arzner directing. I was determined to do each scene to the best of my ability but, with Arzner trying to get me to sit on her lap between takes and insisting on patting and fondling me, I began to freeze up and resent her attentions.

After the picture was finished in June, I went to New York and had a long talk with Jesse Lasky about Arzner, and I never had to do another film with her again.[7]

Despite the rancor at the time, Esther Ralston was quick to admit that Dorothy Arzner was a first-rate director. And Arzner's unorthodox behavior was not held against her by the studio executives. The fact that she dressed in mannish attire, that she made little secret of her sexual preference, that she was, indeed, one of the boys, was if not welcomed, more than tolerated by Paramount's senior personnel. None of the latter are known to have been gay, so their attitude towards Dorothy Arzner was not influenced by their own lifestyles, but rather by a recognition that here was a talented filmmaker who was different—and not frightened or ashamed to let others know that she was not as they were. "I never had any obstacles put in my way by the men in the business," Arzner told Adela Rogers St. Johns back in 1933. "Men actors never showed any prejudice against working with me. All the men who help—cameramen, who are so terribly important—assistants, property men, actors, everybody helped me."[8]

Dorothy Arzner's next film, *Get Your Man*, was her first with the effervescent Clara Bow, who, apparently, was open to any sexual concept. The story involved a Frenchman locked overnight in a Paris waxworks museum with an attractive young American woman. After various plot complications, the two marry, despite the initial objections of their respective families. Playing opposite Clara Bow in *Get Your Man* was a youthful, attractive graduate of the Paramount Acting School, Charles "Buddy" Rogers, who later went on to become the third and final husband of

Mary Pickford, opposite whom he played in *My Best Girl* (1927). "Things were coming so fast for me. They said, would I mind a woman director. I said, 'Mind—nothing,'" Buddy Rogers recalled with all the brashness of eternal youth. "So I remember we had a nice experience. I don't think the picture turned out well, but a lot of them didn't in those days, you know."[9]

"The story has been developed lightly and naturally into a very pleasant little vehicle, and the story is thin enough to permit the introduction of a number of good gags, germane but not essential to the story," wrote *The Moving Picture World* (December 10, 1927). "There is plenty of fun in the waxworks show, some of its obvious, but much that is cleverly contrived, and crucial situations are arrived at naturally and plausibly. Both scenarist and director have contributed to the effect." Completely ignoring the director's contribution, *Variety* (December 7, 1927) opined, "Typical Bow picture that will appease this girl's following. No rave but okay."

Dorothy Arzner's last silent film—it featured a synchronized score and songs by its leading lady, Nancy Carroll— was *Manhattan Cocktail*, released in November 1928. This theatrical melodrama, involves a young couple fresh from college who go to New York in search of employment on Broadway. The boy is eventually killed, and the girl returns home to the safer environment of a small college town and the arms of a waiting professor. *Manhattan Cocktail* was primarily important in helping Nancy Carroll make a successful transition to talkies; it did nothing for Dorothy Arzner's career.

With the coming of sound, Arzner and Clara Bow were reunited in *The Wild Party* (1929), arguably the best of the star's talkies and one of the most outrageous of Arzner's features. It was followed by a further twelve feature films directed by Arzner, of which the best are *Sarah and Son*

(1930), *Merrily We Go to Hell* (1932), *Christopher Strong* (1933), *Craig's Wife* (1936), *The Bride Wore Red* (1937), and *Dance, Girl, Dance* (1940). Arzner's last feature film was *First Comes Courage* (1943). There was never a problem in finding players to work under her direction. Indeed, as child actor Philippe De Lacy, who was featured in *Sarah and Son*, recalled, an appearance in a Dorothy Arzner film was often sought after:

> I was twelve years old, and it did not seem any different or unusual to me to be directed by a woman rather than a man. And don't forget I had been with a lot of top directors, including Lubitsch, Murnau and Ford. I do remember that I wanted the part desperately, and that another young boy was much more favored. However, Dorothy called me in and told me she had selected me for the part.
>
> She was extremely capable, quiet, and she had to deal with a very forceful and temperamental actress in Ruth Chatterton. Dorothy was completely businesslike and straightforward. She never raised her voice. As I say, it never occurred to me that there was anything different in being directed by a woman.
>
> My mother had a great admiration of her, and for her kindness to me. There was a scene where I was in cold water, and she was very concerned that I was kept warm with blankets and so forth. I was enjoying it—it was all a game to me. But then, of course, I enjoyed all my motion picture life, unlike so many people that you read about today.[10]

Little has been recorded concerning Arzner's directorial techniques. The few extant interviews with her deal more in personalities than in the technical aspects of film direction. A little of the vagaries of her style were recalled by

George Folsey, her cinematographer on *Honor Among Lov-*
ers in 1931 and *The Bride Wore Red*, some six years later:

> She was a very interesting woman. I liked her very
> much. She was different from other directors, but not
> complicated or difficult. She never seemed to have
> any trouble, never any problem, with the actors. Of
> course, Joan Crawford could be a little difficult, but
> Dorothy was not someone who could force her opin-
> ions on people.
>
> It was a little difficult to get a set-up out of her. She
> never could make up her mind how she wanted a
> scene shot. After the day's shooting, we would talk
> at night about what we were going to shoot the next
> day, and she would say, "I don't know where we're
> going to shoot it from." I would sometimes get irri-
> tated with her, and tell her there were only so many
> angles anyway. She was very indecisive, but in the
> end we'd get it done. It was fun, except she was so
> hard to pin down.[11]

The four silent films that Dorothy Arzner directed obviously paved the way for the directorial career that was
to follow. They also brought her into contact with a young
woman name Marion Morgan, who staged dances and
other sequences in each of the films. In 1930, the two
women moved into a Hollywood Hills home together and
remained domestic partners until Morgan's death in 1971.
Dorothy Arzner died at her home in La Quinta, near Palm
Springs, on October 1, 1979. As the *Variety* obituary so
sadly stated at its close, "No survivors, no services."

Notes

1. Rob Wagner, in *Rob Wagner's Script*, March 3, 1934, p. 8.

2. This story was told to me by Dix's daughter, Evelyn F. Scott, in a letter dated July 30, 1980. At this time, Scott was working on an authorized biography of Arzner.

3. Gerald Peary and Karyn Kay, "Dorothy Arzner Interview," *Cinema*, no. 34, 1974, p. 10.

4. Quoted in Adela Rogers St. Johns, "Get Me Dorothy Arzner," *Silver Screen*, vol. IV, no. 2, December 1933, p. 24.

5. Quoted in Kevin Brownlow, *The Parade's Gone By*, New York: Alfred A. Knopf, 1968, p. 286.

6. Quoted in Adela Rogers St. Johns, "Get Me Dorothy Arzner," *Silver Screen*, vol. IV, no. 2, December 1933, p. 24.

7. Esther Ralston, *Some Day We'll Laugh: An Autobiography*, Metuchen, NJ: Scarecrow Press, 1985, pp. 106-107.

8. Quoted in Adela Rogers St. Johns, "Get Me Dorothy Arzner," *Silver Screen*, vol. IV, no. 2, December 1933, p. 73.

9. Charles "Buddy" Rogers in an interview with Anthony Slide, *The Silent Picture*, No. 11/12, Summer-Autumn 1971, unpaged.

10. Interview with Anthony Slide, November 1985.

11. Interview with Anthony Slide, November 1985.

Chapter Ten

An Ever-Increasing Number

It seems unlikely that there will ever be an accurate accounting of just how many women worked at one time or another as directors in the American silent film industry. Many directed short subjects which no longer survive and on which there is little written documentation. A considerable number of actresses were given the opportunity to direct at least one film, and several, at their own insistence, did not seek credit. Of the major Hollywood film companies, only Metro-Goldwyn-Mayer, under Louis B. Mayer, was resistant to permitting women to direct, although it did nurture the careers of many prominent female screenwriters in later years, including Zoë Akins, Frances Goodrich, Anita Loos, Dorothy Parker, and Salka Viertel.

A handful of pioneering production companies rewarded their leading ladies with at least one opportunity to direct. At Kalem, Gene Gauntier was the preeminent figure as both actress and screenwriter—except for a short sojourn with American Biograph in 1908—from the company's formation in 1907 until the winter of 1912, when she founded her own company, Gene Gauntier Feature Players. Sidney Olcott was the credited director at Kalem and also served in the same capacity when Gauntier created her own production unit, with the most important early film being the feature-length *From the Manger to the*

Cross (1912), in which Gauntier played the Virgin Mary. Gauntier's contribution as a writer to this and most other Kalem films is well known, yet in 1915, she wrote, "This masterpiece was also conceived, written and co-directed by me, as was *The Colleen Bawn, Arrah-na-Pogue, The Shaughraun, The Kerry Gow, The Wives of Jamestown,* and five hundreds others."[1]

The implication is clear that Gene Gauntier worked as an equal collaborator with Sidney Olcott on the production of all of the Kalem films, at its studios in New York and Jacksonville, Florida, and on location in Ireland, Germany, and the Middle East. Yet, there is only one title, *Grandmother*, released on July 13, 1910, for which Gauntier received published credit as director. The film, a one-reel short, featured Anne Schaeffer (in her first screen role), James Vincent, and Mrs. Julia Hurley, "one of the most famous old ladies of the stage," and according to *The Moving Picture World* (July 16, 1910), "The story centers around the escapades of the pampered son of a wealthy father who falls in love with a popular dancer years older than himself and who is only slightly amused at the young man's ardor."

Kathlyn Williams, the leading lady with the Chicago-based Selig Polyscope Company, is not regarded as a creative force in early filmmaking, but in 1915, she directed, wrote, and starred in a two-reel feature, *The Leopard's Foundling*, released on June 29. The story concerned a white girl, Balu, lost in the African veldt and raised by leopards. She is found by an American hunter (played by Charles Clary), who brings her back to the States, where she must confront civilization and decide whether to stay or return to her jungle home. In the making of the film, Williams took advantage of the studio's collection of "wild" animals, and *The Leopard's Foundling* was filmed at the Selig Zoo, in Los Angeles.

"Women can direct just as well as men," Williams told a 1915 interviewer,

> and in the manner of much of the planning they often have a keener artistic sense and more of an eye for detail—and often it is just one tiny thing, five feet of film maybe, that quite spoils a picture, for it is always the little things that go wrong that one remembers.[2]

Kathlyn Williams continued as a leading lady on screen through the 1920s, at which point she became a character actress, but either by choice or denial, she never directed again.

The Edison Company released a considerable amount of publicity in the summer of 1915 concerning a four-reel production, *A Close Call*, that its leading lady, Miriam Nesbitt, was to direct, write, and star in. Nesbitt visited San Diego, San Francisco, and the Panama Exposition to shoot footage, but there is no record that this film was ever released.

Lucy K. Villa, the wife of director Webster Cullison, directed a number of short subjects for the Eclair Company on location in Arizona in 1914 and 1915.

On December 13, 1913, *The Moving Picture World* announced that

> Mabel Normand, leading woman of the Keystone Co. since its inception, is in the future to direct every picture she acts in. This will undoubtedly make Keystone more popular than ever, and this will give Miss Normand the opportunity of injecting some of her comedy, which she has never had an opportunity to put over before.

The decision by Keystone's Mack Sennett to allow his leading lady (and by all accounts, girlfriend) to direct appears to have been a deliberate slight of the company's new leading man, Charlie Chaplin, who was anxious to write and direct his own comedies, in which Normand was his leading lady. Chaplin was unwilling to accept Normand's direction—"charming as Mabel was, I doubted her competence as a director," he wrote in his autobiography[3]—and Normand was unwilling to accept advice from her leading man.

What actually happened between Normand, Chaplin, and Sennett will never be known, but the outcome was that Sennett allowed Chaplin to direct his own comedies, Normand went back to being a leading lady, but the producer did create the Mabel Normand Feature Film Co. for the making of her 1918 success, *Mickey*.

Every effort to compile an accurate listing of Mabel Normand's directorial credits has proved abortive, in large part because of inadequate contemporary documentation. However, using production data in the Mack Sennett Collection, housed in the Margaret Herrick Library of the Academy of Motion Picture Arts and Sciences, the following is believed to be complete. Dates given indicate when the film was finished or shipped:

Mabel's Strange Affair—December 14, 1913
Won in a Closet—December 30, 1913
Mabel's Bear Escape—January 11, 1914
Mabel's Strange Predicament—January 20, 1914 (with Chaplin)
Love and Gasoline—February 2, 1914
Mabel at the Wheel—March 31, 1914 (with Chaplin)
Caught in a Cabaret—April 11, 1914 (with Chaplin)
Mabel's Nerve—April 30, 1914
Mabel's Busy Day—May 30, 1914 (with Chaplin)

Mabel's Married Life—June 6, 1914 (with Chaplin)
Mabel's Last Prank—August 22, 1914
Mabel's Blunder—August 24, 1914

A lesser comedienne with Mack Sennett was Dorothy "Dot" Farley. In *Illustrated World* (February 1923), Farley claimed to have both written and directed comedies and dramas. While she never worked in a directorial capacity for Sennett, it is possible that she wrote and directed short subjects for some of the other independent production companies for which she worked in the teens and 1920s.

Not as well known and certainly not in the same class as Mabel Normand was Gale Henry, who specialized in eccentric or grotesque comedy roles. From 1915 through 1919, she was the leading comedienne with Century Comedies, and when she left to form her own company, for a one-year period, she wrote, directed, produced, and starred in twenty-six two-reel comedies.

One of the pioneers in the field of clay animation was a woman named Helena Smith Dayton, active in 1916 and 1917. Margaret I. MacDonald, one of a number of women writers on film in the teens and 1920s, discussed Dayton's most prominent production, a 1917 version of *Romeo and Juliet* in *The Moving Picture World*:

Little need be said here of the wonderful talent of Helena Smith Dayton: her work speaks for itself. In the introduction of the picture, we are privileged to watch her deft fingers fashion the form of Juliet from an apparently soul-less lump of clay. This mere lump of clay under her magic touch takes on the responsibilities of life, and love, and sorrow which the play requires, and finally grasps in desperation the dagger with which it ends its sorry life, falling in tragic fashion over the already lifeless body of its Romeo.[4]

The First World War put an end to Dayton's career in films, when, in 1918, she joined the YWCA, serving in France.

The First World War did generate at least one woman filmmaker in government service, and that was Catherine Short, who produced conservation films for the U.S. Food Administration, featuring such popular stars of the day as Marguerite Clark, Elsie Ferguson, and Mabel Normand. According to *The Dramatic Mirror* (May 11, 1918), Short's productions showed "how to save the various commodities most needed by the Government at this time."

In the fall of 1919, D. W. Griffith set up his own studio complex at Mamaroneck, New York. As he was busy in Florida, working on *The Idol Dancer* and *The Love Flower*, he suggested to his leading lady, Lillian Gish, that she should direct the first film at the new studio, a comedy titled *Remodeling Her Husband*, featuring Gish's sister, Dorothy.

Lillian Gish recalled,

He [Griffith] said, "How would you like to direct a picture with your sister? I don't want to break up a happy family, but I think you could do it. I think you know as much about movies as I do." Well, I went home and talked it over with mother and Dorothy to see if they thought it was a good idea. Of course there was no story. Dorothy thought it was all right, and we got a little piece of business Dorothy found out of a funny magazine, and wrote a whole story around that. I asked if I could have Dorothy Parker come and help me with the sub-titles, because she'd never written for the films, but I thought she was so witty and so bright, and I wanted it to be an all-woman picture too. So she did—and then Griffith left with everybody.

He left Harry Carr—he was with the *Los Angeles Times*, an editorial writer, a very brilliant man—and me to do this film I didn't have anybody from the staff to get the studio ready. Well! I had to put in telegraph poles, because we couldn't get enough electricity out on the point. I was taking scenes—it was December— and I'd have Dorothy and James Rennie [the leading man who later married Dorothy] playing the love scene, and it looked as if they were blowing smoke in one another's faces, it was so cold. I then had quickly to go down to New Rochelle and get all my scenery. I had to design all my scenery; there were no set designers. Dorothy helped with her costumes, but I had to see to all the other costumes, see to all the furniture in the sets—you had to do everything.

George Hill was the cameraman, and he was just back from the war, and he had shell shock and was hysterical. And I know I got my main set—the living room—so big and not high enough at the back, so that if he took the whole room in, he shot over the top. He threw his hat in the air, and jumped and stamped on it, and had hysterics about that. I had to keep him calm. Oh, it was terrible.

I had only fifty thousand dollars to make this picture with. We had a scene on Fifth Avenue, and the day before we were to take it, I found you had to have police permit, and it took several days to get. If that happened, I had to have all my crew on salary over the holidays. I said, I just can't; it's too far over the budget. I asked the company and crew if they would take a chance of going to jail with me, because we were doing something illegal. Well, 57th and Fifth Avenue is the busiest section in New York, and I had to have a bus go by a taxi cab, the wife sitting on top of the bus, seeing her husband with a woman in a taxi cab. We had no permit, and we had the cameras in the car ahead, and as we turned, a policeman saw what was happening and held up his hand. Then, he looked at me, and looked again, and then he put his fingers to his mouth and forced a smile [in reference to Gish's actions in her previous film *Broken Blossoms*]. I said, "Yes," and he waved us on and we got by. We finished at 58 thousand dollars and it made, I think, ten times what it cost, which not many films do today.

When Griffith came back, I asked him why he did that to me, had me get a studio ready and make a picture when it was the first one and such an awful chore. He said, "Because I needed my studio built quickly. I knew they'd work faster for a girl then they would for me. I'm no fool." And his studio was ready when he came back. He moved right in, took all his interiors quickly, and released his pictures.[5]

One of the most eagerly sought after of "lost" films, *Remodeling Her Husband* was released on June 13, 1920 to mixed reviews. "If it were not for the inimitable comedy of Miss Gish the feature would be a sorry affair," commented *Variety* (June 11, 1920). *Exhibitor's Trade Review* (June 19, 1920) opined, "Lillian Gish's directorial task is performed in a fashion which gains for her much of the credit attending the picture's success. The continuity is good, the grouping skillful and smooth; swift action prevails throughout." The most interesting comment was made by the distinguished critic Burns Mantle in *Photoplay* (September 1920):

This is a woman's picture. A woman wrote it, a woman stars in it, a woman was its director. And women will enjoy it most. It does an unusual and daring thing; it presents the feminine point of view in plot, in captions, in sets and acting. Our worthy contemporaries of the various trade journals took a good crack at it. They have to take a good crack at something. But at the Rialto in New York, where this review was accomplished, the audience just sat back and howled—and there were men there, too. Lillian Gish has gone back to acting, but we'd like to tell her that she is almost as good a directress as she is an actress—and that's going some. Little things count in this picture; details are not overlooked. Dorothy Gish is just—Dorothy Gish, which is enough for most people. There is no-one like her, and when she gets good stories she should lead her class. James Rennie, recruited from the legitimate, is a gratifying leading man.

It is true that Lillian Gish did not direct another feature, but she was responsible for an important piece of film, and that was the original screen test of a young woman named Lucille Langhanke, who came out to Mamaroneck in the summer of 1920. A harried D. W. Griffith passed her over to Lillian Gish. "She herself directed the test," the actress recalled,

discussing lighting and angles with the cameraman, using reels of film, taking the whole afternoon. I recited bits of poetry, I stood and turned, I walked, I sat and talked to her offcamera. I was completely at ease and happy, for she kept saying, "That's lovely— fine, turn a bit more, pretend I have a puppy in my lap—oh yes! that's beautiful."[6]

D. W. Griffith decided not to sign Lucille Langhanke to a contract, but subsequently, she changed her name and became a major Hollywood star—Mary Astor.

Julia Crawford Ivers is a mystery woman director. No biographical data appears on her in contemporary studio directories. The only photograph of her directing is taken from the rear, with her face hidden. She was born in Los Angeles on October 3, 1867, and took her professional name from her second husband, Oliver Ivers. Ivers's son by her first husband, Frank Van Trees, was the cinematographer James Van Trees. In 1916, Julia Crawford Ivers directed *The Call of the Cumberlands*, starring Dustin Farnum and Myrtle Stedman. Released on January 24, 1916, the film was the second production of the Pallas Company, founded by Frank C. Garbutt, the business partner of Ivers's husband, and a subsidiary of Paramount, which released its features. Of *The Call of the Cumberlands*, *The New York Dramatic Mirror* (February 5, 1916) wrote, "The story is absolutely natural and due to excellent directing its effectiveness is most impressive and the photography is well nigh perfect."

Julia Crawford Ivers was under contract to Famous Players-Lasky as a screenwriter, providing the scripts for many of William Desmond Taylor's films. She was a close companion of the director, identified by fellow screenwriter Grover Jones as "The woman in blue," and with her son, Julia Crawford Ivers visited Taylor's home the morning that his murder was discovered. She wrote another Pallas production, *The Heart of Paula*, starring Lenore Ulrich, shot on location in Mexico and released on April 3, 1916. The direction of *The Heart of Paula* is generally credited to William Desmond Taylor, but it now seems very possible that the film was either directed by Julia Crawford Ivers or co-directed by her with Taylor.[7]

The Heart of Paula was photographed by Ivers's son, as was her third and final directorial effort, *The White Flower*, a Famous Players-Lasky production, released by Paramount in April 1923. A melodrama involving curses and volcanoes, *The White Flower* was filmed on location in Hawaii and starred Betty Compson and Edmund Lowe. Julia Crawford Ivers died in Los Angeles on May 7, 1930. Anyone close to William Desmond Taylor is automatically painted as mysterious, and it might well be that the lack of publicity regarding Julia Crawford Ivers is not because she was an enigma, but simply, in the words of Grover Jones, "a down-to-earth woman"[8] who had little time for the fripperies of Hollywood.

At another Paramount subsidiary, the Jesse L. Lasky Feature Play Company, Camille Astor was a leading lady in the mid-teens, playing opposite Victor Moore in *Chimmie Fadden* and *Chimmie Fadden Out West*, both released in 1915. In 1916, she was appointed as assistant director, with her first film being *The Sowers*, directed by William C. de Mille and starring Blanche Sweet. Astor did not receive credit on this or any other films for which she was the assistant director, nor did she make the grade to director. Another female assistant director was Miriam Meredith, who was a script reader for Thomas H. Ince and J. Parker Read Productions in the late teens, prior to becoming an assistant director with Ince in the early 1920s. Outside of the studio, Meredith founded the Mummer's Workshop Theater in Hollywood, and directed pageants for the Los Angeles YWCA and for the Hollywood Children's Theater Company.

The Russian-born (June 4, 1879, at Yalta, in the Crimea) dramatic actress, Alla Nazimova, formed Nazimova Productions in the early 1920s, a company responsible for two films, *A Doll's House* and *Salome*. Nazimova appeared in some twenty-two feature films between 1916 and 1944 and decided to finance and produce her own films in 1922, after tiring of the productions in which she was starred by Metro. Both *A Doll's House* and *Salome* were commercial failures, and the direction of the films was nominally assigned to Charles Bryant, who had been Nazimova's leading man in eight earlier films and, also nominally, was her husband. (The couple were apparently never legally married, despite Nazimova's calling herself Mrs. Charles Bryant.)

Written by Nazimova under the pen name of Peter N. Winters, *Salome* is an extraordinary stylized film for its day, with its settings and costumes based on the drawings by Aubrey Beardsley that accompanied the first publication of Oscar Wilde's play. As her art director, Nazimova selected Natacha Rambova, who was later to marry Rudolph Valentino and with whom Nazimova shared a Los Angeles home. While there is no question that Nazimova was lesbian, all who know Rambova deny that she was a gay woman, but whatever the relationship between her and Nazimova, there is no question that the latter relied heavily on Rambova's advice in the direction of *Salome*.

The gay and lesbian undertones to the film are so strong that one is tempted to describe it as a "limp-wristed production." One title introducing "Greeks with painted eyes and painted cheeks" is followed by a shot of three very camp-looking, aged Hollywood queens, perhaps the most outrageous moment in a film full of flagrant homosexuality. While praiseworthy for its honesty and integrity, the very elements that make *Salome* popular with modern audiences have tended to obscure its artistic qualities, reducing it to the level of high camp rather than high art.

The emphasis is on the costumes rather than the minimal sets. Wearing a white wig, with what appear to be Christmas ornaments in her hair, and looking far younger than her years, Nazimova, in the title role, exudes a bizarre and erotic beauty. As one critic wrote, she is "like a dove that has strayed; like a narcissus quivering in the wind; like a silver flower." Critical response to *Salome* was mixed at best, with many complaining that the film was nothing more than an excuse for Nazimova to show off various facial expressions. Only the anonymous critic in the *New York Times* (January 1, 1923) displayed a modicum of understanding, commenting, "It is different but does not depend upon mere difference for its attraction."

Aside from *A Doll's House* and *Salome*, it seems likely that Nazimova took a supervisory interest in other productions in which she starred. Ethel Grandin, an actress whose husband, Ray Smallwood, directed Nazimova in *Camille* (1921) and other films, recalls Nazimova's working relationship with her director:

> Ray and Nazimova used to scrap and fight. We'd go down to the beach Saturday and Sunday, and one time we'd fix the lunch and the next time she would bring the lunch. And they would scrap and argue, but they worked out the scenes where they would do it two ways. She liked the fighting, because everybody was "Yes, Madame," and "No, Madame," but Ray wasn't like that. It used to make me nervous when I was near them. It wasn't relaxing. Ray was very upset all the time—it made him nervous working with her.[9]

A Doll's House was released by United Artists on February 12, 1922, with Alan Hale playing opposite the Russian actress. It is interesting to note that Nazimova made her American stage debut in Ibsen's *Hedda Gabler* and had played Nora in *A Doll's House* many times on the stage. Following *A Doll's House, Salome* was released by Allied Producers and Distributors on February 15, 1923. In later years, Nazimova turned to character work. She lived to see her one-time West Hollywood home became a popular hotel for visiting intellectuals from New York, the Garden of Alla, and she died in Los Angeles on July 13, 1945.

Natacha Rambova was the nominal "producer" of two feature films, *What Price Beauty*, and *When Love Grows Cold*. The first was filmed in 1925, under the direction of Thomas Buckingham, and concerned the efforts of two disparate women, a vamp and a simple country girl, to gain the attention of the handsome manager of a beauty parlor. Initial audience response was poor, and the film was not generally released until 1928. *When Love Grows Cold* was shot in 1925, but released in January 1926 concurrent with, and to take advantage of the publicity generated by, Rambova's divorce from Rudolph Valentino. Directed by Harry O. Hoyt, the film starred Rambova as an actress who gives up her stage career to help advance the work of her inventor-husband. When the husband becomes successful, he is lured away from his wife by a vamp, but later the two are reunited. The similarity between the film and Valentino-Rambavo relationship was obvious and helped make of *When Love Grows Cold* a commercial success. Rambova was reportedly outraged by the manner in which the film was promoted, and determined never again to have anything to do with the film industry—a resolution that she kept.

Alice Terry was one of the silent screen's most beautiful and regal stars, particularly in the productions of her husband, Rex Ingram. What is not generally known is that besides looking glamorous, Alice Terry was able to take over direction whenever her husband was feeling out-of-sorts, which would appear to be quite frequently. Despite being under contract to M-G-M, he refused to permit Louis B. Mayer's name on his films, and they were all released as Metro-Goldwyn productions. If by chance, a publicity

Margery Wilson

Margery Wilson and Percy Helton in *The Offenders*, directed by Margery Wilson.

Mrs. Wallace Reid

Bessie Love in *Human Wreckage* (1923), produced by Mrs. Wallace Reid.

Lillian Gish — director

Norma Talmadge and Arthur Edmund Carew in *The Song of Love* (1923), directed by Frances Marion.

Mr. and Mrs. Sidney Drew

Marion Fairfax

Edmund Lowe and Betty Compson in *The White Flower* (1923), directed by Julia Crawford Ivers.

Dorothy Arzner (right) with her first star, Esther Ralston.

Alla Nazimova

item described his films as Metro-Goldwyn-Mayer productions, Ingram would walk off the set in a temper tantrum. Most times, his wife welcomed such behavior as an excuse to stop filming and go to the beach, but when it was inconvenient so to do, she would direct the scene on Ingram's behalf. Alice Terry received no credit for this work, but she is credited as co-director on Ingram's last production, *Baroud*, shot in North Africa and released in the United States in 1933 as *Love in Morocco*. I have Alice Terry's assurance that the bulk of the direction was undertaken by her.

Many of the women directing in the 1920s were screenwriters or playwrights. The most famous was Marion Fairfax, the wife of actor Tully Marshall, who had authored many plays, including *The Builders* (1907), *The Chaperon* (1908), *The Talker* (1912), and *A Modern Girl* (1914). In 1915, she entered the film industry as a screenwriter with the Jesse L. Lasky Feature Play Company, at the suggestion of director William C. de Mille. During the 1920s, in between writing, supervising, and editing more than thirty features, Marion Fairfax found time to direct *The Lying Fool*, a curious production dealing with drug addiction, released by the short-lived American Releasing Corporation on March 16, 1922. As her stars, Fairfax chose Noah Beery, Marjorie Daw, and her husband, Tully Marshall.

Another playwright turned screenwriter, Jane Murfin co-directed (with Justin H. McCloskey) one production, *Flapper Wives*, starring May Allison, and released by Selznick on February 27, 1924. May Tully, the author of a number of undoubtedly second-rate plays, including *Mary's Ankle*, filmed by Thomas H. Ince in 1920, directed two films: *The Old Oaken Bucket* (1921) and *That Old Gang of Mine* (1925). Both productions are probably best forgotten. The scenarist on a number of minor films, Lillian

Ducey directed at least one feature, *Enemies of Children*, a silly melodrama starring Anna Q. Nilsson, released by Mammoth Pictures on December 13, 1923.

Among the one-shot women directors were Vera McCord and Ruth Bryan Owen. The former produced and directed *The Good-Bad Wife*, a very minor film of 1920, featuring Sidney Mason and Dorothy Green. Ruth Bryan Owen, the daughter of William Jennings Bryan, wrote, directed, and starred in an Eastern melodrama, *Once upon a Time*, featuring the Community Players of Coconut Grove, Florida, and released early in 1922. *The Moving Picture World* (January 14, 1922) described the plotline,

> The Shah of an Eastern province is dethroned by a jealous subordinate whose favorite pastime is sending young girls to their death, who fail to amuse him. The most beautiful one of all is not discovered by him until the end and the timely return of the Shah who had survived, despite all belief to the contrary, saves her....It is legendary in style, is a story of indefinite period....the subtitles are written in Biblical phrase.

Once upon a Time was obviously a local Florida production, unrelated to a major studio or any of the major filmmaking centers in the United States at that time. There were similar productions throughout the United States, and at least one such group was directed by a woman. In the early 1920s, Angela Murray Gibson wrote and directed at least nine short subjects, including comedies and dramas, in her hometown of Casselton, North Dakota. When the State Theater in Fargo, North Dakota, opened on November 28, 1921, the first presentation was the Norma Talmadge vehicle, *The Wonderful Thing*, supported by the one-reel comedy, *The Ice Ticket*, written and directed by Gibson. Gibson, who died in 1953, was a graduate of the

Agricultural College (now North Dakota State University), and claimed to have learned production techniques with Carl Gregory at Columbia University and as an assistant director on the 1917 Mary Pickford vehicle, *The Pride of the Clan*.[10]

Madeline Brandeis was another female director working in the American heartland. According to *The Film Mercury* (May 15, 1925), she made at least three independent feature films in Omaha, Nebraska. Whether Brandeis was primarily a producer, a director, or both is not known. The title of only one of the features is on record, and that is *Which Shall It Be?* also known as *Not One to Spare*, released by the W. W. Hodkinson Corporation in June 1924. Madeline Brandeis is credited as producer and Renaud Hoffman as director of the feature, a domestic drama set in Vermont. "One of those tear-compelling little pictures that is going to be a money maker for producer, distributor and the exhibitor," was the opinion of *Variety* (April 9, 1924).

Another multi-talented and long forgotten female director was Elizabeth Pickett, who, after graduation from Wellesley College in 1918, took charge of her family's tobacco farm in Lexington, Kentucky. She next joined the publicity department of the American Red Cross, directing a series of propaganda films and writing eleven hundred of the fifteen hundred pages of *The History of the Red Cross*.

In 1923, Pickett joined the Fox Film Corporation, informing production chief Winfield Sheehan, "I want to write and direct my own pictures."[11] Sheehan took her at her word and sent her back to Kentucky to write and direct a two-reeler, *King of the Turf*. Apparently, John Ford saw the short, liked it, and used it as a basis for his *Kentucky Pride*, released on September 6, 1925, which Pickett edited and titled. *King of the Turf* was to be the first of the Fox

Variety shorts series, of which Elizabeth Pickett became West Coast supervisor and for which she wrote and directed some forty-plus subjects. Aside from the Fox Variety series, Pickett titled and edited several Fox features, including *The Shamrock Handicap* (1926), *Marriage* (1927), and *Fleetwing* (1928). She also wrote the 1929 feature *Redskin*, for Paramount.

With the coming of sound, the era of the female film director, for whatever reason, drew to a close. No definitive explanation can be offered for this state of affairs. Certainly, it was not a sudden close of an epoch. With the advent of the 1920s, there were still women directors, but their impact was less, as was their prominence in the field. While the decade saw the beginning of the career of Dorothy Arzner, there were no major groups of women directors at any studio, and none with the pioneering importance of Alice Guy Blaché or Lois Weber. It was not so much the coming of sound, but rather the 1930s that continued a trend that started in the 1920s. It cost more to make films, and producers were unwilling to take risks with female filmmakers. Mrs. Wallace Reid continued making "B" pictures in the 1930s, because a decade earlier she had proved herself most adept at handling that genre.

Studio production became departmentalized, and the transition from one field of filmmaking to another, from writing to directing or from editing to directing, was more difficult. In general, producers had doubts as to the credibility of directors from the silent era to handle talkies. Not just female directors, but many once-prominent male directors fell by the wayside. New directors were brought to Hollywood from the New York stage—and New York stage directors were usually male. Guilds and unions became firmly established in the 1930s, and these from their inception well into the 1950s and even 1960s were male dominated. An examination of the rolls of the Hollywood Guilds indicates a predominantly male member-ship, with few females holding positions on boards or as officers. Only one female, Mary Pickford, was a primary figure in the establishment of the Academy of Motion Picture Arts and Sciences in 1927, and until the late 1970s, the Academy had only one female president—Bette Davis, for a brief period in 1941.

Because filmmaking was cheaper in Europe, one or two women from the American film industry made the trip to England to work as directors. British-born Elinor Glyn had made an exotic name for herself as a Hollywood screen-writer in the 1920s.[12] In 1929, she formed Elinor Glyn Productions Ltd., rented space at Elstree Studios, and began work on the first of two features she was both to write and direct, *Knowing Men*. Initially written as a star-ring vehicle for Clara Bow—who personified Glyn's ideal of "It"—*Knowing Men* was photographed by Mary Pick-ford's cameraman, Charles Rosher, and starred Elissa Landi and Carl Brisson. Released by United Artists in the United Kingdom in February 1930, the film included a prologue in which Miss Glyn spoke of herself and her art.

Critical response was uniformly bad, with *Variety* (Feb-ruary 26, 1930) commenting, "Said to have cost $150,000. Might have been worth it if it had a story and some direction." *Knowing Men* was followed by *The Price of Things*, again photographed by Rosher, and with Stewart Rome playing opposite Landi. A story of aristocratic twins, *The Price of Things* was again badly received by *Variety* (July 23, 1930): " 'This is awful'—remarked by one of the characters at the end of the film. It certainly was. If a prize were offered for the film containing the most old-fashioned hokum, this one would walk away with it."

Hollywood actress Jacqueline Logan came to Britain in 1931 to write and direct a thirty-seven-minute dramatic short, *Strictly Business*, produced by British International

Pictures and starring Molly Lamont, Betty Amann, and Carl Harbord. Released by Pathé in February 1932, the film received fair notices; *Motion Picture Herald* (March 19, 1932) commented, "The dialogue is clever, the cast competent, making for an entire disregard of the slight length of the picture."

While Americans came to England, at least one British actress, Flora Le Breton, came to Hollywood, and in 1932, she produced a series of twenty-six "hilariously funny" single-reel shorts, released by Fox, and featuring a character called "Crazy Maizie." Also at work in Hollywood as a director was Grace Elliott, responsible for a series of twenty-six, one-reel "Intimate Screen Interviews of Famous Screen Personalities," produced by Talking Picture Epics in 1931. Two of Elliott's interviews—with James Cagney and Mae Clarke—have survived , and dull, static productions they prove to be, containing moments of heavily labored humor, with Dorothy West (not the American Biograph actress) and Paul Power acting as interviewers.

Aside from Dorothy Arzner, the only woman to direct a feature at a major Hollywood studio in the 1930s was screenwriter Wanda Tuchock, who, in 1934, co-directed (with George Nichols, Jr.) *Finishing School* for RKO. Co-authored by Tuchock and starring Frances Dee, Billie Burke, and Ginger Rogers, the film was described by *Variety* (May 1, 1934) as "a combination *Flaming Youth* and *Maedchen in Uniform*."[13]

The American film industry was to remain relatively closed to women filmmakers through into the 1960s, and even in the 1990s, while there may be female directors at work, they are primarily involved in television, and their contributions to the art and craft of filmmaking are irrelevant in comparison to what was accomplished more than seventy-five years ago by Alice Guy Blaché and Lois Weber. If anything, the woman as director survived, after the coming of sound, in Europe, through the brilliant film-making efforts of Leni Riefenstahl and Leontine Sagan, in Germany—Sagan also directed one feature, *Men of Tomorrow*, in Britain in 1935—Germaine Dulac in France, and Olga Preobrazhenskaya and Esther Shub in the Soviet Union.

Notes

1. Letter to Colonel William Selig, dated June 28, 1915, in the Selig Collection at the Margaret Herrick Library of the Academy of Motion Picture Arts and Sciences.

2. "Women Directors Next," *Feature Movie Magazine*, vol. I, no. 3, April 15, 1915, p. 56.

3. Charles Chaplin, *My Autobiography*, New York: Simon and Schuster, 1964, p. 148. Richard Attenborough's shoddy 1992 screen biography, *Chaplin*, makes no reference to Mabel Normand as a director and generally displays an insensitivity toward women that would have been a credit to Chaplin himself.

4. Quoted in Michael Frierson, *Clay Animation*, New York: Twayne, 1994, p. 79. Frierson's book is the only source of documentation on Helena Smith Dayton and contains seven pages on her career.

5. Interview with Anthony Slide, first published in *The Silent Picture*, number 6, Spring 1970, pp. 12-13. There is no proof that *Remodeling Her Husband* was actually written by Dorothy Parker. The credited screenwriter is Dorothy Elizabeth Carter, and this is her only credit. Parker's biographer, Marion Meade, claims that Parker wrote the film, but tells me that her only source was Lillian Gish's autobiography.

6. Quoted in *Lillian Gish*, New York: Museum of Modern Art, 1980, p. 29.

7. Much valuable information on Julia Crawford Ivers and the William Desmond Taylor connection can be found in Robert Giroux, *A Deed of Death*, New York: Alfred A. Knopf, 1980, pp. 96-103.

8. Quoted in Official Report of Proceedings Before the National Labor Relations Board, Los Angeles, October 18, 1937, p. 12.

9. Interview with Anthony Slide, September 10, 1975.

10. Information on Angela Murray Gibson was provided by Ted Larson of Moorhead State University and taken from an article, "Casselton Filmmaker's Legacy Resurrected," by Jim Baccus, in Fargo's *The Sunday Forum*, April 10, 1977.

11. Quoted in Tom Waller, "Elizabeth Pickett," *The Moving Picture World*, vol. 89, no. 7, December 17, 1927, p. 29.

12. For information on Elinor Glyn's career in Hollywood, see Slide, Anthony, *They Also Wrote for the Fan Magazines: Film Articles by Literary Giants from E. E. Cummings to Eleanor Roosevelt, 1920-1939*, Jefferson NC: McFarland, 1992.

13. The work of women directors in the first decade of sound is discussed in Anthony Slide, "The Talkies First Women Directors," *Films in Review*, vol. XXVII, no. 4, April 1976, pp. 226-229.

Appendix A

Woman's Place in Photoplay Production

by Alice Guy Blaché

It has long been a source of wonder to me that many women have not seized upon the wonderful opportunities offered to them by the motion picture art to make their way to fame and fortune as producers of photodramas. Of all the arts there is probably none in which they can make such splendid use of talents so much more natural to a woman than to a man and so necessary to its perfection.

There is no doubt in my mind that a woman's success in many lines of endeavor is still made very difficult by a strong prejudice against one of her sex doing work that has been done only by men for hundreds of years. Of course this prejudice is fast disappearing and there are many vocations in which it has not been present for a long time. In the arts of acting, music, painting and literature, woman has long held her place among the most successful workers, and when it is considered how vitally all of these arts enter into the production of motion pictures one wonders why the names of scores of women are not found among the successful creators of photodrama offerings.

Not only is a woman as well fitted to stage a photodrama as a man, but in many ways she has a distinct advantage over him because of her very nature and because much of the knowledge called for in the telling of the story and the creation of the stage setting is absolutely within her province as a member of the gentler sex. She is an authority on the emotions. For centuries she has given them full play while man has carefully trained himself to control them. She has developed her finer feelings for generations, while being protected from the world by her male companions, and she is naturally religious. In matters of the heart her superiority is acknowledged, and her deep insight and sensitiveness in the affairs of Cupid give her a wonderful advantage in developing the thread of love which plays such an all important part in almost every story that is prepared for the screen. All of the distinctive qualities which she possesses come into direct play during the guiding of the actors in making their character drawings and interpreting the different emotions called for by the story. For to think and to feel the situation demanded by the play is the secret of successful acting, and sensitiveness to those thoughts and feelings is absolutely essential to the success of a stage director.

The qualities of patience and gentleness possessed to such a high degree by womankind are also of inestimable value in the staging of photodrama. Artistic temperament is a thing to be reckoned with while directing an actor, in spite of the treatment of the subject in the comic papers , and a gentle, soft-voiced director is much more conducive to good work on the part of the performer than the over-stern, noisy tyrant of the studio. Not a small part of the motion picture director's work, in addition to the preparation of the story for picture-telling and the casting and directing of the actors, is the choice of suitable locations for the staging of the exterior scenes and the supervising of the studio settings, props, costumes, etc. In these matters it seems to me that a woman is especially well qualified to obtain the very best results, for she is dealing with subjects that are almost a second nature to her. She takes the measure of every person, every costume, every house and every piece of furniture that her eyes come into contact with, and the beauty of a stretch of landscape or a single flower impresses her immediately. All of these things are of the greatest value to the creator of photodrama and the knowledge of them must be extensive and exact. A woman's magic touch is immediately recognized in a real home. Is it not just as recognizable in the home of the character of a photoplay?

That women make the theatre possible from the box-office standpoint is an acknowledged fact. Theatre managers know that their appeal must be to the woman if they would succeed, and all of their efforts are naturally in that direction. This being the case, what a rare opportunity is offered to women to use that inborn knowledge of just what does appeal to them to produce photodramas that will contain that inexplicable something which is necessary to the success of every stage or screen production.

There is nothing connected with the staging of a motion picture that a woman cannot do as easily as a man, and there is no reason why she cannot completely master every technicality of the art. The technique of the drama has been mastered by so many women that it is considered as much her field as a man's and its adaptation to picture work in no way removes it from her sphere. The technique of motion picture photography like the technique of the drama is fitted to a woman's activities.

It is hard for me to imagine how I could have obtained my knowledge of photography, for instance, without the months of study spent in the laboratory of the Gaumont Company, in Paris, at a time when motion picture photography was in the experimental stage, and carefully continued since in my own laboratory in the Solax Studios in this country. It is also necessary to study stage direction by actual participation in the work in addition to burning the midnight oil in your library, but both are as suitable, as fascinating and as remunerative to a woman as to a man.

(Reprinted from *The Moving Picture World*, vol. XXI, no. 3, July 11, 1914, p. 195.)

The Motion-Picture Director

by Ida May Park

Description of Occupation and Qualifications Necessary

The vocation of the motion-picture director is one that commands so comprehensive a knowledge of the arts and sciences, economics and human nature, that it is particularly difficult to describe. To the almost unlimited mental demands on the director is added the necessity of an invulnerable physique. Perhaps that is why the number of consistently successful directors, both male and female, is relatively small. But having these things there is no one, man or woman, who might not take up the profession with a certain degree of confidence in his or her ultimate success.

Because it is so obvious, I have not mentioned the necessity for a well-developed dramatic instinct. Perhaps more than anything else that instinct is the deciding factor of the success or the failure of the motion-picture director. Like acting, this ability to direct is an inborn talent, but it can be cultivated to a certain degree through the mediums of training, proper reading, and environment. But again, as it is with acting, the cultivated art can never equal the natural; it will always lack the fire of genius. From the beginning of the production, when the story is being moulded to scenario requirements, the director is the supervisor, the dominant note of the production, and (I am now writing to women alone) it is her sense of dramatic value that imparts to, or withholds from, the picture that indefinable something which can raise it to the ultimate peak of picture perfection or relegate it to the vast scrap-heap of "rubber-stamp" productions.

Second to this in importance is the artistic eye, for at all times the picture must be perfect in its angles, composition, and grouping. Our chief aim is to please, first and foremost, through the vision.

Preparation Necessary

Preparation, since the demands on knowledge of all kinds is boundless, must necessarily be very general. A college education is a great help if it has not been concentrated on any particular subject to the detriment of others. The whole motion-picture industry is so young and the recognition of the value of good direction so recent that, so far as I know, there is yet no school established which teaches the strictly technical side. Knowledge of camera operation, of lighting effects, and of all the hundred-and-one less important mechanical details must be gained through work in the studio itself. The difficulty of obtaining a position as apprentice or assistant is unfortunately very great.

Opportunity for Advancement

Once in the game the aspirant to a directorship will find the opportunities limitless. Such a statement is not half so extreme as it sounds. The perfect picture is still a thing of dreams. An industry can develop only as the intelligence which directs it develops. The interest of big minds is a thing that until recently has been glaringly absent from the motion picture. But now converts, intelligent converts, are flocking to the banner and results are bound to come in the form of better pictures.

Financial Returns

The financial return is also unlimited. A thousand dollars a week is a small income for a successful director. It might well be called a minimum. There is no maximum.

Advantages and Disadvantages

While production is on there is no rest. No eight-hour day is known to the director. Often work extends far into the night, many times through it, and the next day brings no respite. Given a certain number of weeks, a certain number of dollars, and a troupe of actors, you are under a terrific nervous and physical strain that does not let up until you have completed the work. The obstacles which arise are frequently enough to try the greatest patience. The director must never lose her poise, must never betray the slightest annoyance unless she wishes to jeopardize the success of her picture. In all the world there is no more difficult lot of people to handle than a company of actors. When vacation finally does come, it is never more than two or three days. For the first time in six years I am taking a ten-day vacation, and even now the tentacles of the great cinema octopus reach out at intervals and threaten to drag me back, my vacation half over, into the maelstrom of the studio.

As for the natural equipment of women for the role of director, the superiority of their emotional and imaginative faculties gives them a great advantage. Then, too, the fact that there are only two women directors of note in the field today leaves an absolutely open field. But unless you are hardy and determined, the director's role is not for you. Wait until the profession has emerged from its embryonic state and a system has been evolved by which the terrific weight of responsibility can be lifted from one pair of shoulders. When that time comes I believe that women will find no finer calling.

(Reprinted from *Careers for Women*, edited by Catherine Filene, Boston: Houghton Mifflin, 1920, pp. 335-337.)

Bibliography

Aydelotte, Winifred. "The Little Red Schoolhouse Becomes a Theatre," *Motion Picture Magazine*, vol. XLVII, no. 2, March 1934, pp. 34-35, 85, 88.

Bachy, Victor. *Alice Guy Blaché (1873-1968): La Premiere Femme Cinéaste du Monde*. Paris: Institut Jean Vigo, 1993.

Bertsch, Marguerite. *How to Write for Moving Pictures*. New York: George H. Doran Company, 1917.

Blaché, Alice. "Woman's Place in Photoplay Production," *The Moving Picture World*, vol. XXI, no. 2, July 11, 1914, p. 195.

Bodeen, DeWitt. "Frances Marion," *Films in Review*, vol. XX, no. 2, February 1969, pp. 71-91; vol. XX, no. 3, March 1969, pp. 129-152.

_____. "Wallace Reid," *Films in Review*, vol. XVII, no. 4, April 1966, pp. 205-230.

Carter, Aline. "The Muse of the Reel," *Motion Picture Magazine*, vol. XXI, no. 2, March 1921, pp. 62-63, 105.

Chic, Mlle. "The Greatest Woman Director in the World," *The Moving Picture Weekly*, vol. II, no. 21, May 20, 1916, pp. 24-25.

Denton, Frances. "Lights! Camera! Quiet!" *Photoplay*, vol. XIII, no, 3, February 1918, pp. 48-50.

Drinkwater, John. *The Life and Adventures of Carl Laemmle*. New York: G. P. Putnam's Sons, 1931.

Dunning, Charles S. "The Gate Women Don't Crash," *Liberty*, vol. IV, no. 2, May 14, 1927, pp. 29, 31, 33, 35.

Feldman, Joseph and Harry. "Women Directors — Seem to Go More Often than They Come," *Films in Review,* vol. I, no. 8, November 1950, pp. 9-12.

Francke, Lizzie. *Script Girls: Women Screenwriters in Hollywood.* London: BFI Publishing, 1994.

Gauntier, Gene. *Blazing the Trail.* Unpublished manuscript in library of the Museum of Modern Art, New York.

Gebhart, Myrtle. "Business Women in Film Studios," *The Business Woman,* vol. II, no. 2, December 1923, pp. 26-28, 66-68.

Gish, Lillian. *The Movies, Mr. Griffith and Me.* Englewood Cliffs, NJ: Prentice-Hall, 1969.

Hanson, Patricia King, editor. *The American Film Institute Catalog of Motion Pictures Produced in the United States: Feature Films, 1911-1920.* Berkeley: University of California Press, 1988.

Hark, Ann. "Jill of All Trades," *Ladies' Home Journal,* February 1929, p. 10.

Henry, William M. "Cleo the Craftswoman," *Photoplay,* vol. IX, no. 2, January 1916, pp. 109-111.

"Hollywood Notes," *Close Up,* vol. II, no. 4, April 1928, pp. 54-55.

Hutchinson, Lois. "A Stenographer's Chance in Pictures," *Photoplay,* vol. XXIII, no. 4, March 1923, pp. 42-43, 107.

Jordan, Joan. "The Girl Picture Magnates," *Photoplay,* vol. XXII, no. 3, August 1922, pp. 23, 111.

Katterjohn, Monte M. "Marguerite Bertsch of Vitagraph," *Photoplay,* vol. VI, no. 5, October 1914, p. 160.

Lacassin, Francis. "Out of Oblivion: Alice Guy Blaché," *Sight and Sound,* Summer 1971, pp. 151-154.

Levine, H. Z., "Madame Alice Blaché," *Photoplay,* vol. II, no. 2, March 1912, pp. 37-38.

Lowrey, Caroline. *The First One Hundred Noted Men and Women of the Screen.* New York: Moffat, Yard, 1920.

Marion, Frances. *Off With Their Heads!* New York: Macmillan, 1972.

Martin, Alice. "From 'Wop' Parts to Bossing the Job," *Photoplay,* vol. X, no. 5, October 1916, pp. 95-97.

Mayne, Judith. *Directed by Dorothy Arzner.* Bloomington: Indiana University Press, 1994.

McCreadie, Marsha. *The Women Who Wrote the Movies: From Frances Marion to Nora Ephron.* New York: Carol Publishing, 1994.

Munden, Kenneth W., editor. *The American Film Institute Catalog of Motion Pictures Produced in the United States: Feature Films, 1921-1930.* New York: R. R. Bowker, 1971.

Norton, Helen. "Brains, Brown Eyes and Buttons," *Motion Picture Magazine,* vol. XVII, no. 2, March 1919, pp. 30-31, 105.

Olmsted, Stanley. "Paula Blackton and Her Art," *Motion Picture Classic,* vol. IV, no. 1, March 1917, pp. 52-54.

Osborne, Florence M. "Why Are There No Women Directors?" *Motion Picture Magazine,* vol. XXX, no. 4, November 1925, p. 5.

Owen, K. "Ruth and Her House," *Photoplay,* vol. XII, no. 4, September 1917, pp. 140-142.

Park, Ida May. "The Motion Picture Director," *Careers for Women,* ed. Catherine Filene. Boston: Houghton Mifflin, 1920.

Peary, Gerald, and Karyn Kay. "Dorothy Arzner," *Cinema,* no. 34, 1974, pp. 2-19.

Potamkin, Harry Alan. "The Woman as Film-Director," *American Cinematographer,* vol. XII, no. 9, January 1932, p. 10.

Ralston, Esther. *Some Day We'll Laugh: An Autobiography.* Metuchen, NJ: Scarecrow Press, 1985.

"A Remarkable Monument to Wally Reid's Memory," *Photoplay,* vol. XXVI, no. 4, September 1924, p. 74.

Rogers St. Johns, Adela. "Get Me Dorothy Arzner," *Silver Screen*, vol. IV, no. 2, December 1933, pp. 22-24, 73.

_____, "The One Genius in Pictures—Frances Marion," *Silver Screen*, vol. IV, no. 3, January 1934, pp. 22-23, 53-54.

St. Johns, Ivan. "Good-Bye to Another Tradition," *Photoplay*, vol. XXXI, no. 4, March 1927, pp. 41, 142.

Shane, Maxwell. "Hail the Return of Woman Producer!" *The Film Mercury*, May 15, 1925, p. 8.

Shipman, Nell. *The Silent Screen & My Talking Heart*. Boise, ID: Boise State University, 1987.

Slide, Anthony. *The American Film Industry: A Historical Dictionary*. Westport CT: Greenwood Press, 1986.

_____. *The Griffith Actresses*. New York: A. S. Barnes, 1973.

_____. *The Idols of Silence*. New York: A. S. Barnes, 1976.

_____. *Lois Weber: The Director Who Lost Her Way in History*. Westport, CT: Greenwood Press, 1996.

_____. "Margery Wilson," *The Silent Picture*, no. 17, 1973, pp. 17-24.

_____. "Restoring The Blot," *American Film*, vol. I, no. 1, October 1975, pp. 71, 72.

_____. "The Talkies First Women Directors," *Films in Review*, vol., XXVII, no. 4, April 1976, pp. 226-229.

_____ editor. *The Memoirs of Alice Guy Blaché*, translated by Roberta and Simone Blaché. Metuchen, NJ: Scarecrow Press, 1986.

Smith, Frederick James. "Seeking the Germ: An Interview with the Sidney Drews," *Photoplay*, vol. XII, no. 4, September 1917, pp. 27-30.

Thalberg, Irving G. "Women — and the Films," *The Film Daily*, vol. XXVIII, no. 70, June 22, 1924, p. 29.

Waller, Tom. "Elizabeth Pickett," *The Moving Picture World*, vol. LXXXIX, no. 7, December 17, 1927, p. 29.

Weber, Lois. "How I Became a Director," *Static Flashes*, vol. I, no. 14, April 24, 1915, p. 8.

Williamson, Alice. *Alice in Movieland*. New York: Appleton, 1928.

Wilson, Margery. *I Found My Way*. Philadelphia: J. B. Lippincott, 1956.

"Women Best Fitted to Direct Pictures, Says One of Them," *Camera!* vol. II, no. 39, January 10, 1920, p. 8.

"Women Directors Next," *Feature Movie Magazine*, vol. I, no. 3, April 15, 1915, p. 56.

"Women Film Actors," *The Film Index*, vol. III, no. 38, October 1908, p. 9.

Index